P9-DED-871

THE ART OF RUSSIAN COOKING

THE ART OF RUSSIAN COOKING

Nina Nicolaieff and Nancy Phelan

Drawings by Jules Maidoff

Galahad Books • New York City

Library of Congress Catalog Card Number: 76-57797
ISBN 0-88365-372-9
Printed in the United States of America
Published by arrangement with
Doubleday & Company, Inc.

To our husbands,
Mikhail and Pyotr,
and friends
Pavel and Xenia,
who helped by tasting.

"Hospitality is still . . . one of the chief virtues of the Russian people."

A Handbook for Travellers in Russia.
John Murray. 1875.

CONTENTS

Recipes for items followed by an asterisk may be located by consulting the Index.

AUTHORS' NOTE

Emigré Russians have kept the flag of their native cuisine flying in all parts of the world. This book has been written for people who would like to try Russian cooking, as well as for those who are already familiar with its many attractions. All the recipes can be made with readily available ingredients, apart from a few items stocked at specialty food shops.

We have concentrated on typical everyday recipes and all have been made many times and tested in the best possible way—at the meal table.

Where a recipe calls for bread soaked in milk, then squeezed out, the quantity is measured in wet bread.

Yeast. Dry yeast means dehydrated yeast, which looks like little grains; compressed or fresh yeast looks like putty and is sold by the cake or ounce.

One ounce of dry yeast equals 4 ounces of compressed yeast or 1 cake.

Yeast cannot live at temperatures of below 30° F. or above 90° F., which is why most of its rising must be done before it goes into the oven.

Before starting to make any of the dishes in this book, read the whole recipe through carefully.

INTRODUCTION

The Russian Spirit

"The Russian language has no ascending and descending scale of cordiality . . . only two extremes. If you are not addressed as *brate* (brother) or *galoubchik* (my little pigeon), you are *dourak* or *soukinsine*—terms that I shrink from explaining."

Dumas: *En Russie*

Once a Russian, always a Russian, no matter how long the exile. There is a vitality in the Russian nature that enables emigrés as well as natives not only to retain their own characteristics against all kinds of influences and persuasions but to Russianize most of those with whom they come in contact. This same vitality, which in the past swallowed up foreigners foolish enough to invade the country, is, in its more peaceful form, equally difficult to resist. Sometimes the victim does not even realize he is being swallowed; he is only aware of being enveloped in a warm blanket of exuberant hospitality and goes down without a struggle, calling everyone by diminutive names, eating large meals and drinking vodka like water.

There are nearly 2.33 million Russians in the United States. Even those among them who were born in exile are still intensely Russian. Though the blood may have been watered down the Slav spirit predominates; it flares up at the slightest provocation—a party, an argument, a bottle of vodka; while those who have not diluted their blood still live, think, speak, above all eat Russian among their families and friends.

To the Russian people, eating and drinking are not just a matter of refueling or even of creative achievement but a vital expression of the national spirit. Hospitality is part of their nature, their tradition, their way of life. All through Russian literature writers have let themselves go on the subject of food and drink, lovingly, lyrically, realistically; great eaters have always been admired, great hosts revered. We read of a nobleman "who went through life like a fine old Russian gentleman of the olden time . . . and died of indigestion after a sumptuous dinner at his club." In the past it was normal custom for wealthy Russians to take the cure each year for their livers.

It has been suggested that this spirit of hospitality derives partly from the Moslem reverence for strangers and came through Asiatic peoples assimilated into the Russian empire; but there is also the fact that Russia is so vast, and in the past transport was so bad, that people had to travel great distances to see each other and could only meet infrequently, so they made the most of such occasions. Besides, the winters are so cold that heavy eating and drinking is necessary to keep warm; and Russia is a country that has known great famines. In one twelfth-century famine, conditions were so bad that people ate birch bark, linden leaves, straw and moss, and parents sold their children to foreigners. Even cannibalism was recorded during the thirteenth-century famine in Nijni-Novgorod.

Whatever the cause, Russian hospitality is outstanding.

A Russian meal is an animated affair. Balalaikas vibrate, excited voices argue, declaim poems, propose toasts or break into song. Sooner or later the Russian soul comes up for discussion—they talk of their souls as other nationalities speak of the weather—and some may be overcome and burst into tears, men as well as women. Then kisses and embraces are exchanged, diminutive names used and over all the noise, the music, the emotion is the warm enveloping spirit of Slav hospitality.

Even among the hard-up the same spirit prevails. When funds are low everyone contributes to the feast; but if there were only a herring and a bottle of homemade vodka the Russian character could turn it into a party.

Russian Cuisine

Most Russians, even those who enjoy foreign food, really believe their national cuisine is the best in the world, while the cooking of other countries, if not entirely dismissed or ignored, is regarded with suspicion by the less cosmopolitan. Such prejudices are very high among emigrés, for whom nostalgia and sentiment cloud objective judgment.

Foreigners often think of Russian food as being rich, excessive, exotic. The mixture of races and the country's geographical and climatic differences, added to travelers' tales, descriptions of historic banquets, receptions of tsars, court favorites and rich noblemen of the past, have all helped build this reputation; yet there are any amount of typical Russian dishes that are neither elaborate nor hard to prepare; and it is certain that the common people, the peasants, saw little of splendor or extravagance.

Even among the nobility this lavishness dates only from Peter the Great's time—1672–1725. The early Russian tsars and *boyars* ate very simply, though their food might be served on gold and silver dishes. During the Kievan period—the centuries during which Kiev was capital of Russia—bread and meat were the main items of diet. There was beef, mutton, pork, turkey, fowl, duck, geese, cranes, plus the flesh of wild animals and birds such as deer, wild boar, hare, bear, grouse, hazel-hen, etc. Horsemeat was eaten occasionally but only by soldiers or by civilians during famines.

Food was plainly cooked and presented. (Roast meat or ham garnished with gold paper was considered quite exotic.) There were none of the later sophistications such as capons or milk-fed calves or pigs raised on sweet Hungarian wine; no fresh fish brought from other parts of the country. The custom of transporting live fish in tanks was unknown and there were few "preserve ponds." Even the tsar ate only local or salted fish. Fresh peas, beans and cucumbers were eaten in season and salted cucumbers, plums and lemons, though no capers or olives. Desserts were simple—raisins, currants, figs, prunes, *pastilla* (a fruit-and-honey mixture), apples and pears.

But though plain, food was plentiful. On the tsar's table there might be up to sixty or seventy dishes—on one occasion five hundred—but they were barely tasted and were served purely for etiquette. In fact the ordinary people of Kievan Russia were better fed (and housed) and had more meat than the peasants of Imperial Russia, and were stronger, healthier and more resistant to disease.

After Russia's conversion to Christianity in 988 the Church enforced the Old Testament taboos on meat with blood and birds strangled in snares. The flesh of wild animals was declared "unclean" and forbidden as food. Though the people of Moscow observed these restrictions they were not greatly respected in the country districts. The Church also instituted feasts and proclaimed Wednesday and Friday meatless days; at the same time it encouraged the eating of fish, for those who had access to it. Fish and caviar were very early Russian foods, dating from long before Christianity.

The people also had millet gruel and oatmeal porridge. Eggs, dairy products, vegetables, butter, vegetable oils from flax or hemp seed were used, especially during the long Church fasts, such as Lent.

Bread was always an important part of the diet. In South Russia it was made of wheat flour, in the north usually of rye. In times of famine leaves were added to the flour in an attempt to make it more nourishing.

As well as ordinary bread, there was a special loaf, baked with honey and poppy seeds, for the wealthy and for feast days in monasteries. In *The Life of St. Sergius of Radonezh,* who died in 1392, these sweet loaves are described as "warm and tender . . . and taste exceedingly sweet, as if they had been baked in honey and seed-oil and spices."

Though all food was kept very clean and out of the reach of dogs or other animals, particular care was taken of bread and drinking water. The early Russians regarded bread (and water) with great reverence, an attitude that is believed to descend from Slavic paganism and ancient harvest festivals. Bread is still featured in Orthodox Church rites and in traditional domestic customs of blessing and welcome among the people.

The main drinks of the early Russians were mead and *kvass,* described elsewhere in this book. Wine and vodka were later innovations.

Although Russia has no early literature of cooking, like France, Italy, England and Germany, the old records suggest that meat was either boiled or broiled and vegetables boiled or eaten raw. Corned beef and cured ham are mentioned but no *pirogs* (pies), which later became so popular.

Much of Russia's history may be traced in her cuisine—her conquests, assimilated peoples, treaties and alliances, enemy invasions, the legacies of foreigners who came peacefully and by invitation. In the same way, the country's great physical diversity is seen in materials typical of different areas. As Russia lies between East and West, her cuisine is a union of these two worlds and of influences that range from Scandinavian Northmen to Tartars, Mongols and other Asiatics.

Certain foods and customs were brought from Scandinavia by the Ruriks, invited to rule Russia in the ninth century; others came from Poland, Finland, Lithuania and adjacent Baltic countries. In the south, as Russia invaded the Caucasus, she adopted Georgian, Uzbek, Armenian, Azerbaijan dishes such as *pilaffs* and *shaslik*. Her wars with Turkey, her contacts with Persia may be seen in identical recipes and names of foods in all three countries—though some of the Turkish words and names are relics of the time when this language was spoken at the Russian court. In the Far East, in Siberia, Chinese noodles and *dim sims* (savory fillings wrapped in dough and boiled), had become popular.

The Russians learned of tea from the Chinese, of wine from the Greeks—and later again from Peter the Great, who imported French wines. When St. Vladimir embraced Christianity for Russia further influences came from Byzantium.

In the great houses it was customary to have a highly trained chef in charge of the kitchen. Many of these chefs, who were brought from Turkey or Hungary, gradually added touches and recipes from their own countries to the existing cuisine.

From the reign of Peter the Great European influences

increased, for this brilliant tsar imported whatever he admired in other nations or felt would benefit Russia. As a result of his travels in Europe, Prussian officers, Dutch boatbuilders, English artisans, Italian and French architects and builders were invited to St. Petersburg and with them came Dutch and English dishes, German sausages, schnitzels and sauerkraut, Italian salami, macaroni, ice cream and pastries, French soups and sauces.

During the period of Anglomania, English dishes were very popular. Catherine the Great, who admired French culture, imported many French customs. Though she herself was no gourmet, her grandson, Alexander I, loved French food and in Paris in 1814–15 and at the Congress of Aix-la-Chapelle appointed Carême, the great French cook, to supervise his table. Carême later went to St. Petersburg at the tsar's invitation. He was also chef in the household of the Russian Princess Bagration.

All these influences have resulted in a rich and varied cuisine of which perhaps only a small portion is really indigenous;[1] yet most of the imported dishes have become completely Russianized by the addition of such typical native ingredients as sour cream, dill, mushrooms and salted cucumber.

It is often said that the excessive use of sour cream (*smetana*) makes all Russian food taste the same; yet there is no doubt that it greatly improves certain dishes, giving a rich bland texture to the other ingredients and being far more digestible than many fats. It has a pleasant mild flavor and a creamy consistency. It is essential in certain recipes

[1] Russian influence also worked in reverse, to a certain extent. Not only have great Russian dishes become international; Russian names have gone into foreign menus . . . Orlov, Bagration, Stroganoff, Romanoff, etc.

and if, as the Russians advise, plenty of vodka is taken with meals, the richness is neutralized.

In some countries sour cream is used as a meat tenderizer. It is said to soften the toughest meat in 6 to 24 hours. Its original discovery was probably an accident, due to lack of refrigeration.

Foreign gourmets of the past have spoken harshly of Russian cuisine. Among them was Alexandre Dumas, who spent nine months traveling all over the country in the 1850s; yet though he complained bitterly about the bad cooking he admitted that the raw materials were superb . . . the fish, game, caviar, etc. . . . and the spirit of hospitality above reproach.

Apart from accidental discoveries, characteristic features of national or regional dishes in any country result either from the availability—or special excellence or abundance—of local materials, or from prevailing conditions. In the days before refrigeration, when transport in Russia was slow and infrequent, food was smoked, salted or pickled for preservation and to ensure winter supplies. Summer fruits and vegetables were pickled or marinaded for the months when nothing could grow, fish and meat were salted or smoked for the periods when the rivers and lakes were frozen over. Smoked and salted fish, pickled fruit and vegetables are now typical features of Russian cuisine. The flavors that result have proved so agreeable that these measures, originally taken for necessity, are now carried out for reasons of gastronomy rather than preservation.

Russian Eating Habits

Much has been written of Russian hospitality on the grand scale—of banquets arranged by such nobles as Count

Potemkin, favorite and friend of Catherine the Great, with fountains of wine, pyramids of roasted meat and six hundred covers for the first sitting; of an entertainment given to celebrate the birth of Catherine's grandson Alexander, which cost 50,000 roubles and at which the dessert was set out with jewels worth more than 4,000,000 dollars.

Potemkin, whose lavish tastes helped perpetuate the image of Russian extravagance, ate only the rarest of fruits, the most exquisite of foods. He is said to have bought up a whole greenhouse of cherry trees, in mid-winter, at a rouble a cherry; to have spent 800 roubles ($212.00) a day on his ordinary table, to have hastened his own death by eating, while in a high fever, a meal of salt pork, raw beets, a goose, three or four fowls, with *kvass*, mead and wine. (By contrast, his royal mistress ate and drank very little and went without meat twice a week.)

Such excesses were mainly confined to the upper classes but when occasionally the common people were treated to a banquet they displayed true Russian appetites. At a coronation dinner for subjects, held on the Petrovsky Plains near Moscow, we are told of . . . "8 miles of tables, covered with white cloths . . . sheep roasted whole and dressed in brilliant scarlet jackets, sausages suspended from poles in rich festoons, pies by the thousand, cakes by the tens of thousands."

The food disappeared in record time.

Though the nobility used gold and silver dishes and spoons, gold and silver beakers and bowls for drinking, the early Russians had no forks for eating. Each man used his own knife for cutting meat or bread. Peasants used wooden dishes and spoons, pewter beakers and bowls.

In the noble households of Old Russia the family rose before sunrise for prayers. At eleven o'clock the prince would dine with his retainers, advisers and perhaps visiting priests. At noon, all retired for siesta, and supper was at six.

In more recent times meals fell into four—breakfast, lunch, dinner and a late snack in the evening. Breakfast came to be a light meal of breads and tea, with perhaps eggs; lunch, about midday, was also light . . . fish or vegetables or *pirog* (pie); dinner, eaten between three and five o'clock, became the main meal, preceded by *zakuski* (*hors d'oeuvres*) and vodka, and including soup and *piroshki* (little pies), a main course and perhaps a sweet *tort.* (Most emigrés try to preserve this 3 to 5 P.M. dinner on weekends, even though they have adopted the custom of their new countries during the week.) The evening snack is slight, perhaps taken round the samovar and consisting of cold meats, cheese, bread, sweet preserves or cakes.

These meal hours still prevail in the U.S.S.R. though to a certain extent modified and adapted to changed conditions, to households where everyone, including the mother, goes out to work, to factories or schools where meals are provided in canteens, to snack bars, quick-service cafés and the speeded-up tempo of modern life.

But though hours may vary, the fundamentals of Russian meals remain the same. The dinner table is set with two plates for each person, one on the other; the top plate for *zakuski,* the bottom for the main course. Even if there is no hot course the top plates are removed after the fish *zakuski* are eaten. The table is set with *zakuski,* several different breads—black, rye, white—mustard, plain horseradish and horseradish with sour cream, which is milder.

When the guests are seated and *zakuski* have been passed round, icy-cold vodka is served in small one-ounce glasses.

Traditionally, the hostess sits at one end of the table, exhorting everyone to eat more, and the guests loudly express their approval and admiration of the food. Poultry and meat joints are usually carved in the kitchen and brought in sliced and arranged on a dish. This is a custom viewed with concern by some French chefs and gastronomes. Though they admit its convenience, they complain that it "tends to destroy the fine art of decorating and dressing . . . and indeed to extinguish with one blow the external appearance of our great French cuisine . . ."

The Russians feel it is more important that the food should be easily accessible.

Once the drinks are on the table, toasting is constant. This means that all must drink if they are not to appear unfriendly. In theory, with toasts, all approach the same state of intoxication at the same rate but in fact individual temperaments and different amounts of food eaten make considerable and interesting variations.

In most ordinary Russian households only vodka is drunk at meals but in more sophisticated and cosmopolitan families there is also wine. Some Russians regard wine as a soft drink; others believe that it is dangerous stuff and prefer to play safe with vodka.

In 1568, Master George Turbeville, secretary to an English ambassador in Moscow, wrote of the hospitable Russians as—

Folke fit to be of Bacchus' train, so quaffing is their kind,
Drinke is their whole desire, the pot is all their pride,
The sob'rest head doth once a day stand needful of a guide;
If he to banket bid his friends, he will not shrinke
On them at dinner to bestow a dozen kinds of drinke. . . .

Despite modern changes and a different way of life, this spirit of hospitality is as strong as it was in the sixteenth century.

APPETIZERS
(ZAKUSKI)

Fish, Eggs, Vegetables, Meat

Russian main meals always start with *zakuski.* Even in the most modest household there is some simple dish, if only a herring, to go with a glass of vodka. The *zakuski,* which may be hot or cold, become more elaborate and lavish according to the circumstances of the family. If the main course is to be meat, most of the *zakuski* will be fish, and vice versa.

At an ordinary family meal there may be four or five different *zakuski* dishes on the table. When there are guests —say six or eight—there could be as many as eight or ten *zakuski,* and at parties the only limits are what the host can afford and the table hold.

Typical materials for every day consumption usually include some of the following: *selodka* (salted herring); boiled potatoes with dill; salted cucumber; smoked fish; radishes; sliced salami-type sausages; ham; sardines; sprats; marinaded fish; liver paste; marinaded mushrooms or cabbage; sauerkraut; hard-boiled eggs.

Though, strictly speaking, fruit is not used in *zakuski*, there are certain salads containing apple, which, though dishes in their own right, are often eaten as *zakuski* . . . for instance the Lobster Salad with Vegetables* and Vegetable Salad with Poultry* included in this book. Some hostesses also serve marinaded fruits on the *zakuski* table.

Zakuski, which were brought from Scandinavia by the Ruriks, were introduced to France from Russian in the nineteenth century as *hors d'oeuvres*.

In a country where visitors often came from long distances over bad roads, through snowstorms and other hazards, punctuality was impossible; but guests did not mind waiting for the main meal with appetizers and vodka to sustain them. It has been suggested that these little snacks also helped to slow down the drinking.

Most foreigners have heard or read of Russian *hors d'oeuvres*; they have been the subject of many travelers' tales. These accounts vary—from Dumas grimly tasting "the choicer portion of horseflesh minced with onion, pepper and salt, and eaten raw as an appetizer," offered by a Kalmuck prince, to Sir Harry Luke nostalgically recalling dinners in Tiflis—which never started till at least two hours after the time the guests were invited for—and preceded by fresh caviar from Baku, bears' hams, mushrooms steeped in wine, smoked river trout, salmon and tongue. Then into the next room for hot *zakuski* . . . soup with large game pasties, salmon trout known as *Ishkan*—the Armenian word for prince—kidneys stewed in sour cream and madeira. After all this, to the dining room for the main meal.

Zakuski can be a great trap. When Melba, the famous soprano, went to supper with the tsar . . . very hungry after singing at the opera . . . she innocently and eagerly applied herself to the magnificent buffet, which included every kind of hot and cold *hors d'oeuvre.* She had just reached saturation point when dinner was announced.

This experience, in more modest form, has befallen many unsuspecting foreigners visiting a Russian house for the first time. When you find a table covered with beautiful dishes you naturally assume it to be the main meal. Too late you discover that soup with *piroshki* and pork fed for weeks on Hungarian wine are waiting in the kitchen till appetites have been suitably stimulated.

The Russians laugh kindly at protests but expect you to go on eating, like the host in Gogol's *Dead Souls,* who rebuked his guest for lack of appetite. . . . One cannot have only one chicken leg on the plate for everything must go in pairs; and it cannot be left at two—it must be three because of the Holy Trinity—and when the guest cries that he has no more room the host reminds him that when His Excellency enters a crowded church a little more room can always be made by moving up. . . .

The only solution for those of poor appetite invited for a Russian meal seems to be several days fasting beforehand.

FISH ZAKUSKI
[Ribniye Zakuski]

Salted Herring
[Selodka]

Selodka is popular at any time of the year. It may be served in many different ways, with garnishes, with eggs, on black bread, with salads and so on; but it is probably best eaten with hot boiled potatoes, well buttered and sprinkled with dill, chives or spring onions.

1 salted herring
1 white onion
Oil and vinegar

To prepare, soak the herring in cold water for 8–10 hours; then cut off the head, slit stomach and clean out intestines. Wash under cold running water. Cut down the center of the spine, through to the bone and starting at the top, peel the skin away, one side at a time.

Take out the backbone and cut the fish across in ½-inch pieces. Arrange it on a long plate, like a whole fish. Put rings of white onion on top and sprinkle with oil and vinegar. 6–8 *servings*

Salted Herring in Mustard Sauce

[Selodka s Gortchitzei]

*1 salted herring, soaked, cleaned and cut as for Salted Herring**
1 tablespoon ready-mixed mustard
3 tablespoons oil
1 white onion

Garniture:

1 hard-cooked egg, finely chopped
Chives or spring onion, chopped

Mix mustard and oil together. Slice the onion into fine rings and mix in lightly with the oil and mustard. Cover and leave 30 minutes.

Spread the mixture over the herring and leave for 1 hour. Serve sprinkled with finely chopped hard-cooked egg and chives or spring onion. *6–8 servings*

Herring Potato Salad

[Kartofelinii Salat s Selodkoi]

*2 salted herring fillets soaked, cleaned and cut as for Salted Herring**
3 cups sliced cooked potato
½ cup sliced dill pickle
½ cup chopped hard-cooked egg
½ cup sliced white onion
¼ cup oil
White pepper to taste
Salt to taste

Garniture:

1 hard-cooked egg
Chives or spring onion

Mix 1 sliced herring fillet with the potatoes, dill pickle, egg, onion, oil, pepper and salt, taking care not to break up any of the ingredients.

Pile the mixture in the center of a plate and arrange around it the second fillet, cut into ½-inch pieces, with rings of hard-cooked egg and chives or spring onion.

This salad could also be served on a long dish. When cleaning the herring, keep the head and tail. Arrange salad in the shape of a fish, put head and tail at the ends, decorate top with second fillet cut into ½-inch pieces, rings of onion and hard-cooked egg. Sprinkle with chopped chives or spring onion. *6–8 servings*

Marinaded Fresh Fish in Tomato Sauce

[Marinovanaya Riba v Tomatiye]

1½ pounds fresh firm-fleshed fish such as snapper, cod, bass
Salt
½ cup plain flour
½ cup oil
1 cup sliced onion
¾ cup tomato sauce
¾ cup water

Optional: 1 cup shredded carrot

Bone and cut the fish into pieces about 1 by 2 inches. Salt them, roll in flour. Heat the oil in a frying pan and fry the fish till brown. Remove, and keep hot in a saucepan while you fry the onion in the same oil. Fry till light brown.

Add the tomato sauce diluted with ¾ cup water to the onions and bring to a boil. Pour hot mixture over the fish and simmer for 5–10 minutes. Chill for ¾ hour. Serve cold.

This *zakuska*, which is very good, is even better if you add 1 cup of shredded carrot to the onion and lightly fry them together. The carrot gives a sweet and mellow taste to the fish. *6–8 servings*

Fish in Aspic

[Zalivnoe iz Riba]

1½–2 pounds fresh firm-fleshed fish such as flounder, pike, cod
1 teaspoon salt
1 bay leaf
½ teaspoon peppercorns
1 small onion
2½ cups water
1 tablespoon gelatin
1 hard-cooked egg, sliced

Garniture:

1 hard-cooked egg, sliced
Dill or parsley
*Horseradish and Sour Cream Sauce**

Scale, clean and wash the fish.

In a saucepan put the salt, bay leaf, peppercorns and onion, with 2½ cups of water, and bring to a boil. Add the whole fish and boil for 10–15 minutes. Remove from the heat. Take out the fish, skin it and take the flesh from the bones. Cut it into small pieces.

Strain the fish stock and add the gelatin.

Rinse a 4-cup oval mold with cold water. On the bottom arrange a pattern with one sliced hard-cooked egg, then put in the fish and pour the aspic over it slowly. Chill until the liquid is set—approximately 4–5 hours. Unmold, garnish with the second sliced hard-cooked egg and dill or parsley. Serve with horseradish and sour cream sauce.

This recipe may be used for a whole fish. It is also good as a basis for a more elaborate party dish in which a fish-shaped mold is used and decorated.

As in the preparation of any aspic dishes, it will be easier to arrange the decorations if you first pour a little of the liquid aspic into the mold. *6–8 servings*

Hot and Cold Smoked Fish

[Kopchenaya Riba]

In Russian recipes the terms *hot-smoked fish* and *cold-smoked fish* refer not to the temperature at which they are eaten but to the manner in which they are smoked. *Hot-smoked fish* are slightly salted, first baked and then smoked at a temperature of 176° F. from one to five hours. The fire used is of aromatic wood, such as pine or oak. Hot-smoked fish does not keep as long as cold-smoked fish and should not be stored for more than a day or two without refrigeration.

Cold-smoked fish is salted, then soaked, dried and put into a smoke chamber at a temperature of 104° F. It will keep much longer, in the same way as smoked ham.

In this book, hot-smoked fish used are eel and trout; cold-smoked are cod, haddock and salmon.

Cold-smoked Fish Salad

[Salat iz Kopchenoi Ribi]

½ pound smoked cod or haddock
2 tablespoons oil
1 tablespoon ready-mixed mustard
Dash pepper
½ cup finely sliced onion

Garniture:

2 tomatoes, sliced
1 hard-cooked egg, sliced

Remove skin and bones from the fish and cut into very thin slices. Carefully blend together the oil and mustard, adding the oil gradually as for making mayonnaise. Add pepper. Lightly mix together the fish, onion and sauce. Cover and leave for 2–3 hours. Serve in a shallow dish, decorated with sliced tomato and egg. *6 servings*

Hot-smoked Fish

[Kopchenaya Riba]

1 smoked fish, such as trout, about 1–1½ pounds
1 ten-ounce can asparagus spears
*½ cup Mayonnaise**

Remove skin and bones, and fillet fish. Cut into ½-inch pieces and arrange on a long plate, in the shape of a whole fish. Arrange asparagus spears on top and mask with mayonnaise. *6 servings*

Smoked Eel

[Kopchenii Ugor]

Smoked eel
Lettuce leaves

Smoked eel, which is bought from specialty food shops, is rather rich and fat and needs no mayonnaise. Simply take off the skin and remove the backbone, then cut the fish into ½-inch pieces. Arrange on lettuce leaves on a crystal plate.

Smoked Salmon

[Kopchenaya Semga]

Like caviar, smoked salmon is too good to be messed about with. Cut it into paper-thin slices and eat with black bread or buttered toast.

Salted Canadian pink salmon can be eaten the same way.

Lobster Salad with Vegetables

[Salat iz Omara s Ovoschami]

1 cooked lobster, weighing about 2 pounds
3 hard-cooked eggs, chopped
3 cups, cut into ½-inch dice, boiled potatoes
1 cup diced fresh cucumber
1 cup diced fresh apple
1 cup cooked, fresh, frozen or canned green peas
1 cup asparagus pieces
1 teaspoon salt
White pepper to taste
*1½ cups Mayonnaise**

Garniture:

Lobster shell
1 hard-cooked egg
Radishes
Asparagus
Dill or parsley
Olive oil

Take the meat out of the lobster without breaking the shell. Cut into cubes, mix gently with three of the eggs, the potato, cucumber, apple, peas and asparagus. Add the salt, pepper and mayonnaise. Pile it all up in a long dish, arranging the lobster shell and legs on top of lobster and salad mixture and decorating all round with rings of hard-cooked egg, radishes, asparagus, dill or parsley. Brush the shell with olive oil to make it shine.

This makes a good centerpiece for a cold buffet party table. *6–8 servings*

Lobster, Crab or Prawn with Mayonnaise

[Omar, Krab z Mayanezom]

1 cooked lobster
Large lettuce leaf
*Mayonnaise**

Clean the meat from the shell, arrange it on a lettuce leaf and cover with mayonnaise, partly or completely, according to taste. *4–6 servings*

Anchovies on Egg
[Anchovies s Yaitzami]

Eggs, as required
Stuffed or filleted anchovies

Garniture:

Lettuce
Tomato
Parsley

Hard-cook as many eggs as you need; cut them into rings and put stuffed or filleted anchovies on each ring. Arrange on a plate, decorated with lettuce, tomato and parsley.

Fresh Fish Caviar Spread
[Ribnaya Ikra]

½ pound fresh soft roe, such as mackerel or shad
¼ cup oil
1 teaspoon salt
1 tablespoon lemon juice or vinegar
Pepper to taste

With a fork, remove the skin from the roe, put roe into a deep bowl and mix with the fork, picking out all the tissues till the roe is absolutely clean. Add oil, salt, lemon juice or vinegar and pepper. Mix until completely blended and put into a glass dish.

Serve with small pieces of black bread or on rings of hard-cooked egg.

If more salt is added this spread will keep for 2 to 3 weeks in the refrigerator. The roe of any fish can be treated in the same way. *4 servings*

Caviar

[Ikra]

Caviar is the most famous of all *zakuski.* We do not know how or exactly when the Russians began eating it but it is one of their oldest foods. Nor do we know how it came to be called caviar. Some authorities believe the word is of Tartar origin, others that it comes from the Turkish *Khav-yah,* which is said to derive from the Italian *Caviale.* The Russians themselves call it *Ikra,* with the accent on the second syllable.

It soon became appreciated in other countries. The Greeks, who received it through their trade with the present Kuban district, regarded it as a great delicacy; and in Elizabethan England it was so esteemed as to be almost a symbol of exclusiveness. Shakespeare, in Hamlet, speaks of "caviar to the general," meaning "above the heads of the crowd."

The preparation and transportation of caviar are very expensive, which is why it is still a luxury. It is sold either fresh or pressed.[1] The former, which is the greater delicacy, is soft and more perishable than pressed caviar. When pressed

[1] Both fresh and pressed caviar are available through The Iron Gate, 424 W. 54th St., N.Y., N.Y. 10019.

it is very black, the eggs are harder and it travels well, which is why it is more often encountered outside Russia than fresh caviar.

There are three grades of black caviar. The best and most expensive is *Beluga*, which is actually pale gray, with large eggs about the size of buckshot; *Sevruga* is also pale gray but the eggs are smaller; and *Ossetrina*, which has quite small eggs, is a darker gray. Experts claim they can tell which area the caviar comes from by its flavor.

These so-called black caviars are the roe of the sturgeon, but there is also a red caviar which comes from the salmon. It has large translucent eggs, like miniature bubbles, orange in color and very salty. Though it is cheaper than black it is very good and highly nutritious.

Brillat-Savarin says that caviar "rouses the instinct of reproduction in either sex."

Though most of us regard it as a luxury, in Russia compressed caviar is used as army rations because of its highly concentrated nutritional value and because it keeps for long periods. Russian cooks also use caviar, pounded and diluted with cold water, for clarifying soups; while red caviar is dried and used as fuel by peasants during the salmon breeding season in such areas as the Amur River, where the whole waterway becomes blocked with masses of these orange eggs.

There are two good rules for buying and eating caviar: buy the very best you can afford; and eat it plain, on buttered toast or bread or with *Blini**, (Russian pancakes). It should always be kept very cold and served in a suitably elegant crystal dish, if possible one which has a pocket for ice.

EGG ZAKUSKI

[Yaitchniye Zakuski]

Savory Eggs

[Farscherovaniye Yaitza]

6 hard-cooked eggs
2 tablespoons butter
Salt and pepper to taste
2 tablespoons anchovy paste
3 small tomatoes, sliced

Cut the eggs in halves. Carefully take out the yolks and blend smoothly with the butter, salt, pepper and anchovy paste. Fill the egg white with this paste, using a teaspoon or better still a pastry or icing tube. Put a half slice of tomato on each egg and arrange on a dish.

These savory eggs may be varied by using herring, caviar, tomato sauce, salmon, fish paste, curry or any other flavor instead of anchovy paste. *6 servings*

Eggs with Horseradish Sauce

[Yaitza s Hrienom]

6 hard-cooked eggs
*½ cup Mayonnaise**
½ cup sour cream
1 tablespoon horseradish
Salt
Pepper

Cut eggs in halves and put into a 2-inch-deep glass or crystal dish. Mix the rest of the ingredients together and pour over the eggs about 30 minutes before serving. *6 servings*

Grilled Half-eggs
[Pechoniye Yaitza]

6 large hard-cooked eggs
1 tablespoon butter
2 tablespoons chopped dill
¼ teaspoon salt
Pepper to taste

Cut eggs—still in shells—in halves. Remove any small chips. With a teaspoon carefully take out yolks and whites, trying not to break shells. Put eggs in a dish and mash up with a fork. Add butter, dill, salt and pepper. Mix well. Put the mixture back into the shells and grill under a medium heat for 5–10 minutes, watching all the time, as they burn easily. Serve hot or cold. *6 servings*

VEGETABLE ZAKUSKI
[Ovoschniye Zakuski]

Stuffed Green Peppers
[Farscherovanii Pierietz]

4 or 5 medium-sized green peppers
½ cup oil for frying
1 large onion, chopped
1 pound carrots, shredded
½ cup tomato sauce
½ teaspoon salt
Pepper to taste
½ cup water

This is a very simple but extremely good *zakuska.*

Prepare the peppers by cutting off the tops and taking out the seeds. Make the stuffing by frying the onion, then adding the shredded carrots and frying together for a few minutes. Add the tomato sauce, salt and pepper. Put the mixture into the raw peppers, put them into a saucepan with the water and simmer, covered, for 20 minutes or until cooked. Serve cold.

Optional:

Extra peppers could also be cut up into strips, ½ inch by 1 inch, and mixed with the filling; or ½ cup of cooked rice could be added to the stuffing. *6–8 servings*

Poor Man's Caviar

[Baklajanaya Ikra]

1 medium-sized eggplant
Enough water to cover eggplant
½ cup chopped onion
½ cup vegetable oil
½ teaspoon salt
Pepper to taste
¼ cup tomato sauce

Cook the eggplant in water for about 15 minutes. Drain it, peel off the skin and chop it very fine.

Fry the onion in oil until golden brown. Add the eggplant, salt, pepper, tomato sauce. Mix together and simmer for 5–10 minutes. Cool. Put it into a glass dish and serve cold. Excellent on black or white bread. *6 servings*

Eggplant with Vegetables

[Baklajan s Ovoschami]

1 small eggplant
½ cup chopped onion
½ cup vegetable oil
1 cup finely diced carrots
1 cup chopped fresh tomato
1 cup finely diced squash
½ teaspoon salt
Pepper to taste
½ cup water

Peel the eggplant and cut it into cubes. Fry the onion in oil till light brown. Add eggplant and the rest of the ingredients except the water and fry for 5 minutes. Add water and simmer in covered saucepan for 30 minutes. Serve cold. *6–8 servings*

Stewed Vegetables

[Tuschoniye Ovoschi]

2 large squashes, about 1 pound each
3 medium-sized white onions
½ pound green beans
½ pound carrots
½ cup oil
½ cup water
Pepper to taste
1 teaspoon salt

Garniture:

Dill
Chives or spring onion

Peel squashes and onions and cut into rings. Cut the beans into sections, diagonally. Peel and shred the carrots. Arrange all in a casserole in layers, starting with the squash. Mix together the oil, water, pepper and salt. Pour over vegetables. Bring to the boil, then cook, covered, for 30–45 minutes on low heat. Allow to cool. Put into a glass dish and sprinkle with dill, chives or spring onion.

This may be served hot or cold. When cold it is used as a *zakuska,* when hot as a garnish for meat. *6–8 servings*

Vegetable Salad
[Vinegret]

This salad, served without meat and with mayonnaise, is usually called Russian Salad by non-Russians.

For Dressing:

½ cup oil
¼ cup vinegar

For Salad:

2 cups cooked diced potatoes
1 cup cooked diced beets
1 cup cooked diced carrots
½ cup salted diced cucumber
¼ cup finely chopped onion
½ cup fresh diced apple
Salt to taste
Pepper to taste

Alternative Dressing:

*Sour cream or Mayonnaise**

Garniture:

Lettuce leaves
1 hard-cooked egg

Mix together oil and vinegar, if using this dressing; then put all salad ingredients into a bowl, add chosen dressing and mix all together carefully, trying not to break up the diced vegetables. Put into a glass dish or plate and arrange lettuce leaves round. Make a daisy pattern on top, using whole yolk of egg for center and cutting whites to make 6 to 8 petals. Serve cold.

Optional:

To make a more substantial dish, add any cold meat, poultry or fish pieces or finely chopped herring. *7–8 servings*

Potato Salad

[Kartofelnii Salat]

3 cups cold cooked sliced potatoes
½ cup sliced white onions
2 hard-cooked eggs, chopped
*1 cup sour cream or Mayonnaise**
Salt
Pepper to taste

Garniture:

Dill

Mix all the ingredients together lightly, put into a salad dish and garnish with dill. *6–8 servings*

Sauerkraut

[Kvaschenaya Kapusta]

2 cups sauerkraut
¼ cup vinegar
¼ cup vegetable oil

Garniture:

Spring onion or parsley

Mix well and leave for 10 minutes. Put into a glass dish and decorate with spring onion or parsley. *4 servings*

Radishes with Sour Cream

[Rediska v Smetaniye]

2 cups washed and finely sliced radishes
½ cup sour cream
Pinch salt

Mix all together but not till 5 minutes before serving, otherwise the radishes will give out juice and make the sour cream watery. *4 servings*

Fresh Spring Salad

[Zelyenii Salat]

1 head lettuce
1 cucumber
6–8 radishes
Dill
Spring onions

For Dressing:

½ cup sour cream
1 teaspoon sugar
½ teaspoon salt

Garniture:

Dill

Wash and cut the lettuce, not too fine. Peel and slice the cucumber. Slice radishes in thin half-slices. Chop dill and spring onions. Mix all together.

Combine sour cream, sugar and salt and leave for 3–4 minutes. Just before serving, pour mixture over the salad, mix lightly and sprinkle with dill.

This salad is often used as accompaniment for meat dishes. *6 servings*

MEAT ZAKUSKI
[Myasniye Zakuski]

Tomato and Meat Salad
[Pomidori s Myasom]

3–4 medium-sized tomatoes
1 cup cold cooked pieces meat . . . veal, lamb, beef, pork or chicken, or mixture of all
½ cup ham
1 hard-cooked egg
*¼ cup Mayonnaise**
½ teaspoon salt
Pepper to taste
3–4 radishes

Garniture:

Lettuce leaves

Wash tomatoes, cut off tops and with a sharp teaspoon remove the centers. Set empty tomatoes upside-down to drain off juice.

Cut the cold meat and the ham into fine straws, about 1 inch long. With egg cutter, slice off 3–4 rings of hard-cooked egg—one for each tomato—and chop the rest of the egg very fine. Mix together meat, ham, chopped egg and mayonnaise. Add salt and pepper to taste. Fill the tomato cases with this mixture and put one ring of hard-cooked egg on top of each. Make Radish Roses* and set one on each egg slice. Serve arranged on a plate of lettuce leaves. *3–4 servings*

Radish Roses

Cut the red skin of the radish in 4 or 5 sections to about halfway down the radish, then gently, with knife point, ease the section of cut skin away till it stands up like a petal. Cut carefully and not too deeply into the radish.

Veal Brawn

[Holodetz]

2 veal shanks
1 onion
2 carrots, peeled
1 bay leaf
1 teaspoon salt
Pepper to taste
Enough cold water to cover shanks
1 teaspoon gelatin
½ cup cooked green peas
1 hard-cooked egg

Garniture:

Parsley
*Radish Roses**

Put the veal shanks with the whole onion, carrots, bay leaf, salt and pepper, into saucepan of cold water; bring to boil and simmer until the meat starts to separate from the bones. Remove the carrots and meat, strain the stock and add the gelatin. Take the meat off the bones and cut into small pieces. Make a pattern with the cut-up carrots, cooked peas and rings of hard-cooked egg on the bottom of a 6-cup mold, which has been rinsed out with cold water. Put the meat on top and add the stock very carefully, trying not to disturb the pattern. Chill until set, about 4–6 hours, then unmold and garnish with parsley and radish roses.

This recipe could also be used for pig's trotters or pig's head, chicken or goose giblets and hearts, instead of veal shanks. *6–8 servings*

Liver Paste

[Paschtet]

1 pound chicken livers
¼ cup chopped onion
8 tablespoons butter
¼ teaspoon salt
Pepper
½ cup cool boiled water or meat stock if needed

Wash and clean the livers of all tissue. Fry the onion lightly in 2 tablespoons butter. Add livers, salt and pepper and fry with onion for 5 minutes; then cover frying pan and simmer until liver is cooked through. Watch carefully that it does not become too dry. If this happens add ¼ cup water or stock.

Put the mixture with 4 tablespoons butter through a meat grinder two or three times. Mix all together. If it seems too dry add a little of the cool water or stock. Pile the liver paste on a plate in a pyramid and garnish with the remaining 2 tablespoons butter, softened, forcing it through an icing tube. *4 servings*

Homemade Ham

[Vetchna Domaschnaya]

1 leg fresh pork
1½ pounds plain flour
1 teaspoon salt
Water

Ask the butcher to pump the leg some hours before you are going to cook it, and hang it to drain for about 2 hours. It is best to order the meat in advance, which gives the butcher time to pump and drain it.

Preheat oven to 350° F.

Mix the flour, salt and enough water to form a thick

dough. Roll out and wrap round the meat. Bake for about 30 minutes to the pound. If it is a very young pig, 20 minutes to the pound should be enough.

Take it out of the oven and let it cool; then remove the flour-and-water case, peel the skin back halfway, pin it down with cloves or decorated toothpicks.

This ham is delicious hot. When eating it hot take the dough off when it comes from the oven, brush the skin with butter or fat and put back into the oven to brown. *Approximately ½ pound per serving*

Tongue in Aspic

[Zalivnoe iz Yazika]

1 fresh ox tongue
Enough stock or water to cover it
2 carrots, peeled
1 onion
1 bay leaf
½ teaspoon peppercorns
1 teaspoon salt
2 tablespoons gelatin
½ cup hot water
1 hard-cooked egg

Garniture:

Lettuce
*Horseradish Sauce**

Clean away all the tough parts of the tongue, wash it well, put it in a saucepan and cover with meat stock or water. Add whole peeled carrots, onion, bay leaf, peppercorns and salt. Bring to a boil, then simmer, covered, until tongue is tender, approximately 30 minutes to the pound.

Leave the tongue to cool in the stock; then take it out, skin it and cut into ¼-inch slices or dice. Take out the carrots and cut into slices. Strain the stock. Melt 2 tablespoons gelatin in ½ cup of hot water and add to 4 cups of the stock.

Rinse out a 10-inch round mold with cold water. Pour in a little of the aspic. Cut egg in slices and arrange in a pattern with carrots in this aspic. Allow to set for 10 minutes, then arrange the sliced or diced tongue in a circular pattern, one layer on another until all is used. Pour over the aspic and chill till firm, about 4 hours. Unmold on a large plate, garnish with lettuce and serve with horseradish sauce. *8 servings*

Pot Roast in Aspic

[Zalivnoe iz Myasa]

The better the beef, the better this dish.

2–3 pounds beef—tip or rump roast—in one piece
1½ teaspoons salt
Pepper to taste
1 tablespoon fat
2 medium-sized onions, chopped
1 bay leaf
2½ cups boiling water
1 tablespoon gelatin
½ cup hot water

Garniture:

2 hard-cooked eggs
2 cups cooked fresh or canned green peas
1 cooked carrot, diced
1½ cups potato straws
1 tablespoon sour cream

Wash the meat and rub it all over with the salt and pepper; then brown it on all sides in the fat in a skillet, put it into a saucepan and add the chopped onions and bay leaf. Swill out the skillet with 2½ cups boiling water and pour over the meat. Bring to a boil, then simmer, covered, for

2 hours. When cooked it should be very tender but not stringy.

Strain the stock from the saucepan, add some more water to bring it up to 2½ cups again. Allow to cool. Melt the gelatin in ½ cup of hot water. Add to beef liquid. Cut the meat into pieces about the right size for serving. Arrange rings of hard-cooked egg on the bottom of a 6-cup ring mold that has been rinsed with cold water. Pour a little aspic over them and leave to set for half an hour. Put in the pieces of meat and pour the rest of the aspic over it carefully. Leave to set for 3–4 hours. Unmold, put peas and diced carrots in the center and potato straws all round. Serve cold.

A spoonful of sour cream on the peas and carrots looks attractive and tastes good. *8 servings*

Vegetable Salad with Poultry

[Salat s Kuritzei]

1 cooked stewing fowl, about 3 pounds
3 cups diced boiled potatoes
½ cup diced cooked carrots
½ cup cooked green peas
½ cup diced apple
½ cup peeled and diced fresh cucumber
½ cup chopped hard-cooked egg
*1 cup Mayonnaise**
Salt
Pepper to taste

Garniture:

1 hard-cooked egg, sliced
Few slices cucumber and carrot
Black olives
Lettuce leaves
Dill

Cut the fowl meat into dice, reserving the breast, which is used for garnishing. Mix all the ingredients together very carefully. Put them into a dish or on a flat platter and decorate with egg, cucumber, carrot, olives, lettuce, dill and pieces of fowl breast.

This salad is often known among Russians as *Salat Oliviye.* *8–10 servings*

HOT ZAKUSKI

[Goryachiye Zakuski]

Crab and Rice Croquettes

[Risoviye Kroketi s Krabom]

*2 cups cold Boiled Rice**
1 six-ounce can crab meat
2 tablespoons butter
4 eggs
½ teaspoon salt
½ cup plain flour
½ cup bread crumbs
2 cups oil for deep-frying

Garniture:

Chopped parsley

Put the rice into a mixing bowl, open the can of crab meat, pour the juice into the rice and put the crab through a mincer. Add minced crab to rice. Add the butter. Separate eggs, and add yolks to rice and crab. Taste for salt. Mix well; then with floured hands roll into small balls—or croquettes—about the size of a Ping-Pong ball. Lightly beat the egg whites. Dip the croquettes into the egg white, then roll in bread crumbs. When all are ready, heat the oil to 400° F. and deep-fry for 3–5 minutes, till golden brown. Arrange on a plate, sprinkle with chopped parsley and serve hot. *4 servings*

Fish Fillets with Sour Cream

[Riba v Smetaniye]

1 pound best fish fillets such as flounder, cod, pike
½ teaspoon salt
½ cup plain flour
½ cup oil
½ cup milk
1 cup sour cream

Wash the fillets and dry them on a cloth. Salt them and roll in flour. Heat oil in skillet and fry fillets on both sides till light brown. Remove excess oil from the pan. Mix together milk and sour cream. Pour over the fillets, bring to a boil and serve immediately. *3 servings*

Chicken Livers in Sour Cream

[Pechonka v Smetaniye]

1 pound chicken livers
2 tablespoons butter
1 small onion, finely chopped
1 teaspoon salt
Pepper to taste
1 cup sour cream

Prepare livers by washing and removing unwanted skin tissue. Cut each in half, melt the butter and fry the chopped onion. When light brown, add the livers. Add salt and pepper. Fry for 10–15 minutes but do not let them get dry. Pour in the sour cream, bring to a boil and serve hot. *4 servings*

Other *zakuski* suggested:

- Beef and Herring in Bread Crust*
- Cottage Cheese Spread with Caraway Seeds*
- Stuffed Tomatoes*
- Poultry Kotletki*
- Fried *Pelemeni**
- Boiled Fowl Fried in Bread Crumbs*
- Marinaded Cabbage*
- Marinaded Fruit*
- Salted Cucumber*
- Fried Mushrooms*
- Egg Croquettes*

SOUPS

(SOUPI)

Russia has a variety of soups, thick and thin, hot and cold, sweet and savory. A number of these are adaptations from other countries . . . the cream and purée types from France, the cold fruit soups from Germany or Scandinavia, others from the Caucasian countries; but some are peculiarly Russian, such as the fish soups, notably the famous Sterlet Soup, *Borsch* and *Schi* (Cabbage Soup). All these are known outside Russia, if not from restaurant menus, then from Russian literature.

HOT SOUPS

[Goryachiye Soupi]

The best-known hot soup outside Russia is *Borsch*, but many people do not realize that there are a number of varieties. To most non-Russians *Borsch* is a red liquid made of beets and served with sour cream, for this is the type usually served in restaurants. Though beets are always included, all *Borsch* is not red.

It is made in many different ways with different ingredients—with beef, bacon, frankfurters, duck, vegetables. In the winter it could be made with sauerkraut, brown beans, root vegetables and mushrooms; in spring with young beet leaves instead of cabbage.

We have given four of the most popular recipes, all good, but perhaps the first two, made with beef, are best. Meat *Borsch* is a meal in itself. The soup is drunk, then the beef eaten separately, with mustard or horseradish; or sometimes the meat is eaten first. Since it is not worth making this soup for less than eight, people often get together for *Borsch* parties, especially in winter. It is not hot-weather food.

Leftover soup could be used next day, for it improves with keeping; or it can be frozen and eaten a week later.

Borsch parties should start with *zakuski*, which should not be too filling—no potato salads or heavy dishes, though *piroshki* (little pies) could be served with the soup instead of bread. The emphasis should be on fish *zakuski*—herring, sprats with eggs, eel, caviar and perhaps Salted Cucumber* —in view of the meat and vegetable to come. If bread is served it should be black, and if *piroshki* are eaten they should be made with meat or cabbage filling.

Borsch

Few beef bones
5-pound piece fresh beef brisket
1 clove garlic
2 bay leaves
1 tablespoon salt
Pepper to taste
Enough water to cover meat and bones
1 onion
1 small cabbage
3 medium-sized carrots
1 small parsnip
3 medium-sized beets
3 medium-sized potatoes
1 cup tomato purée
½ cup sour cream

Wash the bones and put them into a big saucepan with the meat, garlic, bay leaves, salt and pepper. Cover with water, bring to boil, then simmer, covered, for 1 hour.

Meanwhile prepare all the vegetables—peel and chop the onion, cut the cabbage into 1½–2-inch chunks, peel and cut carrots, parsnip and beets into thin strips, 2 inches long. Peel and cut potatoes into ½-inch dice.

Take out meat and bones from saucepan and strain the liquid through a fine sieve. Put meat back into liquid, add all the vegetables, except the potatoes. Bring to a boil and simmer, covered, for 45 minutes. Add tomato purée and diced potatoes. Simmer for another 30 minutes. Serve with a teaspoon of sour cream in each plate.

When serving meat separately do not forget to put horseradish and mustard on the table. *8–10 servings*

Moscow Borsch

[Moskovskii Borsch]

This is the famous red *Borsch.*

All ingredients as for Borsch* plus
1 pound bacon, in 1 piece
1 tablespoon oil or bacon fat
1 extra beet

Wash the meat and bones, put them into a big saucepan with garlic, bay leaves, salt and pepper. Be careful with salt, since bacon is salty. Cover with water, bring to boil and simmer for 1 hour.

Meanwhile prepare vegetables—peel and chop the onion, cut the cabbage into 1½–2-inch chunks, peel and cut carrots, parsnip and the 3 medium-sized beets into thin strips, 2 inches long. Peel and cut potatoes into ½-inch dice.

When the meat and bones have simmered for 1 hour take them from the saucepan and strain the liquid through a fine sieve. Put the meat back into the saucepan, add the strained broth and the cabbage.

Cut the bacon into ¼-inch dice and fry in oil or bacon fat for a few minutes. Add the cut-up vegetables, all except potato, and fry for 10 minutes with the bacon. Add to the broth, bring to a boil, then simmer for 45–55 minutes. Add tomato purée and diced potatoes and simmer, covered, another 20–25 minutes.

To give the extra deep red color the additional beet is shredded and fried quickly for 5 minutes in remaining oil or bacon fat, then added to the *Borsch* just before serving. One teaspoonful of sour cream is put into each plate. *8–10 servings*

Vegetarian Borsch

[Postnii Borsch]

1 onion	*1 clove garlic*
1 small cabbage	*2 bay leaves*
3 medium-sized carrots	*6 cups water*
1 small parsnip	*1 cup tomato purée*
3 medium-sized beets	*Pepper to taste*
3 medium-sized potatoes	*Salt to taste*
2 tablespoons oil for frying	

Peel and chop the onion, cut the cabbage into 2-inch chunks, peel and cut carrots, parsnip and beets into thin strips, 2 inches long. Peel and cut potatoes into ½-inch dice.

Lightly fry in the oil the onion, carrots, parsnip and beets. Put them into a saucepan with garlic and bay leaves and cover with 6 cups water. Add the cabbage, potato and tomato purée, pepper and salt. Simmer, covered, until the vegetables are soft, about 1 hour.

This is the *Borsch* served during Lent. *6 servings*

Borsch, Navy Style

[Flotskii Borsch]

1½–2 pounds bacon or ham bones
1 clove garlic
2 bay leaves
Enough cold water to cover bones and make a broth
1 onion
1 small cabbage
3 medium-sized carrots
1 small parsnip
3 medium-sized beets
3 medium-sized potatoes
½ cup oil for frying
1 cup tomato purée
Pepper to taste
Salt to taste
1–1½ pounds frankfurters
1 tablespoon butter
½ cup sour cream

Make a broth by putting bacon or ham bones into saucepan with garlic and bay leaves. Cover with cold water; bring to a boil, turn down the heat and simmer, covered, for 45 minutes.

Prepare vegetables. Peel and chop onion, cut cabbage into 2-inch chunks, peel carrots, parsnip, beets and potatoes and cut into slices, not strips.

Fry vegetables in oil and add to the broth when it is ready and has been strained. Add tomato purée and simmer, covered, for 30 minutes. Add pepper and salt, tasting carefully before adding salt, since broth from the bacon or ham bones will already be salty. Just before serving cut the frankfurters into 1-inch pieces, fry lightly in butter, add to soup and boil up for 3 minutes. Serve with sour cream. *8 servings*

Kidney and Cucumber Soup

[Rassolnik]

Some Russians make this soup thick, but it is excellent when very light and delicate.

1 ox kidney
Cold water for cooking kidney
1 teaspoon salt
2 carrots, peeled
1 onion
1 parsnip, peeled
8 cups chicken broth
Dash pepper
1 bay leaf
3–4 potatoes, diced
*3–4 small Salted Cucumbers**
Water to cover cucumbers
½ cup sour cream
1 hard-cooked egg
Chopped dill or parsley

Wash the kidney thoroughly and put it in cold water to cover. Bring it to a boil and boil for 10 minutes. Drain off the liquid and in fresh water to cover with 1 teaspoon of salt boil it again until tender. Leave it in the water.

Cut the carrots, onion and parsnip into small dice and add to the chicken broth with pepper, bay leaf and extra salt if necessary. Cook, covered, over medium heat for 20 minutes. Add diced potatoes and simmer another 20 minutes. Cut salted cucumbers in dice, put in separate saucepan, cover with water and cook on low heat for 10 minutes.

Add cucumbers and liquid to rest of the soup. Take the kidney out of the water and cut in small dice. Add it to the rest of the ingredients and bring all to a boil for 5 minutes.

Put the sour cream in a bowl, add crushed, hard-cooked egg and mix them together. Before serving, put 1 teaspoon of this mixture into each plate and pour the soup over it. Sprinkle with chopped dill or parsley. 6 *servings*

Spring Soup or Green Soup
[Zelyonii Soup]

- *6 cups chicken or beef bouillon*
- *½ pound young carrots, scraped*
- *1 small parsnip, scraped*
- *1 small onion*
- *1 tablespoon butter or margarine*
- *Salt to taste, if bouillon is not already salted*
- *½ pound young potatoes*
- *1 bunch sorrel*
- *3 hard-cooked eggs*
- *½ cup sour cream*
- *Dill or parsley, chopped*

Bring the bouillon to boiling point.

Cut the carrots, parsnip and onion into slices, then half slices. Fry lightly in butter or margarine, add to the boiling bouillon, season if necessary and simmer for 10 minutes. Add the potatoes, cut in dice. Simmer for 15 minutes. Wash the sorrel thoroughly and chop fine. Add to the soup and boil for another 10 minutes.

Serve ½ hard-cooked egg and 1 teaspoon of sour cream in each plate of soup. Sprinkle with dill or parsley.

If no sorrel is available, spinach, fresh or canned (2 cups), could be used. *4–6 servings*

Georgian Soup

[Kavkaskii Soup]

The stock for this Caucasian soup could be made with the raw lamb bones left over after meat has been cut off for *Shaslik**.

1½–2 pounds lamb or mutton shoulder and shank chops
6 cups stock or cold water
1 tablespoon salt
Pepper to taste
Bay leaf
1–2 cloves garlic
2 carrots, peeled
1 onion
1 stalk celery
1 small green pepper
½ hot chili pepper
2–3 potatoes
2–3 tomatoes
1 cup elbow macaroni

Put the chops into stock or cold water with salt, pepper, bay leaf and garlic. Bring to a boil, then simmer, covered, for about 40 minutes. Strain the bouillon through a sieve, take the meat out and remove the bones.

Dice the carrots, onion, celery, green pepper, chili pepper and add to the bouillon and boil on low heat for 30 minutes. Put back the meat into the soup. Dice the potatoes, skin and chop the tomatoes, and add both, with the macaroni, to the other ingredients. Simmer for 30 minutes more. Serve with pieces of the meat.

To avoid a greasy soup, trim all the fat from the meat before cooking. If you have time, as a further precaution, let the soup get cold and skim off any fat that forms on the surface before heating to serve. *4–6 servings*

Cabbage Soup
[Schi]

"Schi i kasha pischa nasha" . . . "Cabbage soup and *kasha* (buckwheat) is our daily food."

This is a very old and famous saying, known to thousands of Russian peasants and soldiers. *Schi* is a very typical Russian soup and is often mentioned in the literature of the country. With black bread, it is usually synonymous with the plainest of living. In his autobiography, the seventeenth-century priest Avvakem mentions, while in prison, being given "a little bread and cabbage soup to eat." It "tasted good."

Foreigners are sometimes less enthusiastic. The fastidious Dumas considered it "infinitely inferior to anything our poorest farmer would send out to his field workers"; but the Russians still talk enthusiastically about their *Schi.* At its worst a thin tasteless concoction, when properly made it is a nutritious, well-flavored and satisfying dish.

It is made with sauerkraut or with fresh cabbage or with half of each. It can be made with meat stock and served with boiled beef or with pork or on its own. Some people add tomatoes.

½ pound sauerkraut
1 small cabbage
1 onion
1½ teaspoons butter or beef fat
1 carrot, peeled
7 cups beef bouillon
2–3 potatoes
½ cup tomato purée or 1 cup fresh tomatoes
Salt to taste
½ teaspoon peppercorns
Bay leaf
½ cup sour cream
*Boiled Buckwheat** (kasha)

Wash the sauerkraut and cabbage in cold water and drain thoroughly. Chop the onion and fry in the butter or beef fat. Cut the carrot into slices, then halve the slices and add to onion. Fry lightly. Add the cabbage and sauerkraut, cover pan and simmer for 30 minutes, with a little bouillon or water, watching to see it does not burn.

Add the rest of the bouillon. Cook on low heat until the cabbage is tender. Cut the potatoes into ½-inch dice and add, with tomato purée, salt, peppercorns and bay leaf. Taste carefully for salt as there is salt in the sauerkraut. If using fresh cabbage only, use more salt.

Serve, adding 1 teaspoon sour cream to each plate, and if you like it, boiled buckwheat (*kasha*) in a separate dish. *4–6 servings*

FISH SOUPS

[Ribniye Soupi]

Russia has a great variety of fish soups, some of them unique in that the materials are not found outside the country. One famous example is Sterlet Soup, which Russians have always prized greatly and which in the past was the preserve of the rich and the nobility because of its high price. Though Dumas commented rather caustically that this was the only remarkable thing about it, it was always regarded as a supreme delicacy. Certain restaurants prided themselves on the quality of their Sterlet Soup, especially the celebrated Troitza Restaurant in Moscow, owned by the Troitza Monastery. This restaurant's only monastic touch was that though patrons could eat and drink as much as they liked the doors of the private rooms must not be shut.

In Russia, the stock for fish soups is made from sea or river fish, which should be as fresh as possible.

Sterlet Soup could be made, using the recipe for Fish Soup (*Ouha*) given below, with the main difference that gourmets demand the sterlet be alive when brought into the kitchen.

Fish Soup

[Ouha]

2 pounds fresh fish such as cod or pike
7 cups water
Bay leaf
1 tablespoon salt
1 teaspoon peppercorns
1 carrot, peeled
1 parsnip, peeled
1 onion
2–3 potatoes
Chopped dill or parsley

Boil the fish in the water with the bay leaf, salt and peppercorns for 8–10 minutes. Drain off the fish stock into another saucepan and add the carrot, parsnip and onion, cut in slices, and potatoes cut in dice. Boil for 20 minutes.

Remove all bones and skin from the fish and put it back into the soup. Simmer for 5 minutes more and serve with dill or chopped parsley on top.

Ouha should be accompanied by Hot Salmon Pie* or Pie with Fish Filling*. *6 servings*

Fish Soup with Salted Cucumber
[Solyanka]

7 cups chicken broth
1 cup peeled diced carrots
1 onion
1 tablespoon salt
Pepper to taste
Bay leaf
1½ cups diced potatoes
¼ pound pitted green olives
1½ pounds fish such as snapper or pike, with bones removed
2 cups boiling water
*2 Salted Cucumbers**
2 lemons

Bring the broth to a boil. Add the carrots, onion, salt, pepper and bay leaf. Simmer for 15 minutes. Add potatoes and cook on low heat another 15 minutes. Add olives.

Put fish into separate saucepan. Pour over it 2 cups boiling water and simmer, covered, for 5 minutes. Drain off water. Cut fish into pieces 1 by 2 inches, and add to soup. Cut cucumbers into half slices and add. Bring to a boil and simmer for 5 minutes. Cut one lemon in thin slices and serve one slice in each plate. The other lemon is cut in sections for squeezing and is served on a separate dish. *6–8 servings*

COLD SOUPS
[Holodniye Soupi]

These may be sweet or savory. They are excellent in summer and are served very cold. Since the ingredients are chopped up and kept in the refrigerator till the last minute all preparations could be done early in the day, or the day before, and the *Kvass** or wine which makes the liquid added just before serving.

Cold Kvass *Soup*
[Okroshka]

3 hard-cooked eggs, chopped
1 cup boiled diced potatoes
½ cup diced radishes
1 cup peeled and diced fresh cucumber
1½ cups diced cold meat—beef, poultry, lamb or ham
½ cup chopped green onions or chives
1 teaspoon salt
2 sprigs dill
4 cups Kvass*
2 tablespoons sour cream
6 ice cubes

Mix together all ingredients except *kvass,* sour cream, ice cubes and a little of the dill. Put into refrigerator. Five minutes before serving pour cold *kvass* over the chopped mixture and mix in lightly. In each plate put 1 teaspoon of sour cream, one ice cube and a sprinkle of dill. 6 *servings*

Cold Kvass *Soup with Crab Meat or Lobster*

[Okroshka s Krabom ilie Omarom]

This is prepared and served exactly as Cold *Kvass* Soup*, using the following ingredients:

1 eight-ounce can crab meat, drained and chopped in small pieces
4 hard-cooked eggs, chopped
1 cup peeled and diced fresh cucumber
1 cup diced boiled potatoes
½ cup chopped green onions or chives
1 teaspoon salt
Sprig dill
4 cups Kvass*
2 tablespoons sour cream
6 ice cubes

6 servings

Cold Beet Soup

[Svekolnik]

4 medium-sized young beets, with leaves
½ cup water
1 teaspoon vinegar or lemon juice
½ cup diced cooked carrot
1 cup diced cooked potato
1 cup peeled and diced fresh cucumber
2 hard-cooked eggs, chopped
Salt and sugar to taste
5 cups Kvass*
2 tablespoons sour cream
Dill

Wash and peel beets and cut into strips. Cut the stalks into ½-inch pieces. Put in a saucepan with the water, vinegar or lemon juice and simmer for 30 minutes.

Wash and shred the beet leaves. Add to the beets and

simmer for 10 minutes. Chill; then mix in with the carrot, potato, cucumber, eggs, salt and sugar. Five minutes before serving add the cold *kvass.* Serve with 1 teaspoon of sour cream and a little dill in each plate. *6 servings*

COLD SWEET SOUPS

[Holodniye Soupi, Slatkiye]

There are a number of these soups made from all kinds of fruits or berries. Some have become so sweetened to the Russian taste that they are almost like desserts, but this can be adjusted by reducing the amount of sugar.

Cold Apple Soup

[Yablochnii Soupi]

3 pounds apples
Few cloves
Peel ¼ lemon
As many soft bread crumbs as you want for thickening —the quantity depends on how thick you want it
1 cup water
½ cup sugar
1 tablespoon raspberry jam
1 teaspoon lemon juice
1 bottle sweet white wine

Peel, core and slice the apples. Put them in a saucepan with the cloves, lemon peel, bread crumbs and 1 cup water; bring to a boil, then simmer till soft. Mash well and add the sugar, jam, lemon juice and the white wine. Serve very cold.

Dry red wine could be used instead of white, in which case you will need to add an extra ½ cup of sugar. *6 servings*

Fresh Berry Soup
[Yagodnii Soup]

3 cups fresh berries—raspberries, blackberries, gooseberries or black currants (plums could also be used)
4 egg yolks
½ cup sugar
1½ cups fresh cream
Extra sugar if berries are very sour

Wash and clean the berries and put them through a sieve, mashing them to a pulp. Mix the egg yolks with the sugar and one-third of the mashed-up berries. Put into a double boiler and heat almost to boiling point but do not boil. Mix in the rest of the berries.

Whip the cream, pour it into the soup, mix well and serve. May be eaten hot or cold. *4 servings*

FISH

(RIBA)

In a country with as many rivers, lakes and seas as Russia . . . Baltic, Arctic, White Sea, Black Sea, Caspian Sea, Sea of Azov . . . fish is naturally an important part of the diet, and this is encouraged by the frequent fasts of the Russian Church, during which meat is forbidden.

Fish is always available, for in winter when the lakes and rivers are frozen there are smoked and salted supplies. Many people in the inland areas have probably never tasted fresh sea fish at all.

In the past certain fish were highly prized, especially the fresh-water sterlet, which many non-Russians consider over-rated. Rich nobleman went to extravagant lengths to obtain it for soup. This fish, which is found in the Volga and other southern rivers, can only live in its native water and at a certain temperature, and since it must be perfectly fresh it was transported alive across country in special trucks fitted with fish tanks. In summer the tanks of river water were shaded from the sun, in winter they were fitted with slow ovens for warming. At elegant St. Petersburg dinner parties the guests would be shown the sterlet, alive and swimming, which they would later eat as soup.

For fish not obtainable outside Russia, local substitutes may be used—for instance snapper instead of sturgeon.

The Russians say that since fish spend their lives in liquid they should do the same in death, water being replaced by vodka.

The nourishing properties of fish are well known. Brillat-Savarin goes further, claiming that a fish diet in general stimulates the reproductive system and increases virility.

Baked Fish with Egg

[Pechonaya Riba s Yaitzami]

2 tablespoons butter
1 tablespoon fine bread crumbs
4 best boneless fillets of fish, such as pike, mullet or white perch
¾ teaspoon salt
6 eggs
½ cup milk
Dash pepper
Chopped dill or parsley

Preheat oven to 350° F.

Butter a shallow oven-proof dish and sprinkle it with fine bread crumbs. Wash, dry the fish with a clean cloth, salt it, reserving some salt for later, and put it in the dish. Put a little butter on top of each fillet and bake in moderate oven (350°–400° F.), until it is almost cooked . . . about 10–15 minutes.

Beat the eggs with the milk. Add the rest of the salt, the pepper, chopped dill or parsley. Pour it over the fish and bake till there is a golden-brown crust on top. Serve immediately.

This recipe may also be cooked in smaller individual oven-proof dishes. *4 servings*

Sturgeon
[Sterliad]

Though this is a famous and typical Russian fish, it is available in the U.S.A. It is best when young for as it gets older its flavor becomes less delicate. If it is inclined to be hard it will be improved by marinading beforehand in white wine. This marinade, with herbs and seasoning to taste, can then be used for cooking the fish.

Sturgeon à la Russe
[Sterliad po Russki]

*1 Salted Cucumber**
½ cup cold water to cover cucumber
1 onion
1½ tablespoons butter
½ pound mushrooms
1 carrot, peeled
1 parsnip, peeled
Few capers
½ cup tomato sauce
1½ pounds sturgeon or snapper
Salt
Water to cover sturgeon
1½ pounds cooked potatoes

Garniture:

2 lemons
Chopped dill or parsley

Cut the cucumber into long thin strips. Cook on low heat in very little water for 5–10 minutes. Slice the onion and fry it in butter and add the roughly cut up mushrooms, the carrot and parsnip cut in strips. Fry all together for 5 minutes, then add capers, tomato sauce and the cooked cucumber. Simmer for 10 minutes. Keep hot.

Cut the sturgeon meat into four pieces, put in a saucepan with a little salted water and bring to boil. Simmer until cooked, about 10 minutes. Take the fish out of the water, put it on the serving dish, pour vegetable mixture over it and surround it with cooked potatoes. On each piece of fish put a section of lemon and sprinkle the whole with chopped dill or parsley. *4 servings*

Poached Fish Polonaise

[Riba po Polski]

This is a Polish recipe adopted by the Russians.

2 pounds whole fish or a section of a big fish such as snapper, pike or cod
Enough cold water to cover fish
1 teaspoon salt
6–8 peppercorns
2 bay leaves
2 tablespoons butter
3 hard-cooked eggs, chopped
1½ pounds boiled potatoes

Garniture:

Chopped dill
Chives

Put the fish in a saucepan with water, salt, peppercorns and bay leaves. Bring to a boil, then draw to the side of the heat and keep liquid just simmering till fish is cooked. In another saucepan melt the butter and while still hot mix with the chopped hard-cooked eggs. Take the fish from the water, put it on a warm serving dish, arrange potatoes round it and cover the whole with the egg and butter mixture. Sprinkle with chopped dill and chives. *4 servings*

Fish Kotlet *with Mushroom Sauce*

[Ribniye Kotletki s Gribnim Sousom]

2 pounds boned fish, such as cod, pike, carp
1 cup torn, soaked in milk, then squeezed out white bread
1 egg
1 teaspoon salt
Pepper to taste
¼ pound butter
Bread crumbs
1 cup oil for frying

Sauce:

1 small onion
1½ tablespoons butter
½ pound mushrooms
1 tablespoon flour
½ teaspoon salt
½ cup milk
1 cup sour cream

Chop the fish finely and add the soaked bread, beaten egg, salt and pepper. Take 1 tablespoon of the mixture at a time and roll it into a ball. Insert ½ teaspoon of butter in the middle and flatten the *kotlet* to ½ inch thickness. Roll in bread crumbs and fry in oil. Keep hot.

To make the sauce, chop the onion and fry it in butter, adding the mushrooms, which have been well washed and coarsely chopped. Fry together till the mushrooms are cooked. Sprinkle the flour over them, mix well together and add the salt and the ½ cup of milk. Bring to a boil. Remove from the fire and 5 minutes before serving add the sour cream. The sauce may be served separately or poured over the *kotletki*. *4 servings*

Fish Gratin

[Kokil]

2 pounds boneless fish fillets, such as carp, pike, flounder
1 teaspoon salt
½ cup plain flour
½ cup oil
½ cup cooked green peas
½ cup diced cooked carrot
1 cup hard-cooked egg, chopped
1 tablespoon capers
*2 cups White Sauce**
2 tablespoons mature grated cheese, such as Parmesan

Preheat oven to 350° F.

Wash the fish, salt it and roll in flour. Fry in hot oil, until light brown. Drain and cool for 5–10 minutes.

Break up the fish, not too small, and put it in an ovenproof dish. On the top of the fish put the peas, carrot and chopped egg. Mix the capers into the white sauce and pour over the fish. Sprinkle grated cheese on top and bake for 15–20 minutes. (May also be made in individual dishes.)

4 servings

Fish with Squash and Sour Cream Sauce

[Riba s Kabachkom v Smetaniye]

2 pounds boneless fish cutlets, such as halibut or flounder
1 teaspoon salt
Pepper
½ cup flour
1 cup oil for frying
1½ pounds squash
2 cups sour cream
¼ cup grated cheese, such as Parmesan
¼ cup bread crumbs

Garniture:

Chopped dill

Preheat oven to 350° F.

Prepare the fish by salting, peppering and rolling in flour. Drain. Reserve some salt and flour for squash. Fry till light brown in ½ cup oil. Put in an oven-proof dish that can be brought to the table. Cut the squash into slices, take out the seeds in center, salt and roll the slices in flour, then fry them on both sides in remaining oil till golden brown. Put the squash on top of the fish and pour over the sour cream. Mix the grated cheese with the bread crumbs, sprinkle over the dish and bake in a medium oven until a golden-brown crust forms—about 15 minutes. Serve with chopped dill sprinkled on top. *4 servings*

Treska *in White Wine and Rice*

[Treska v Bielom Viniye s Risom]

2 pounds fish fillets, such as snapper or bass
1 teaspoon salt
Pepper
½ cup butter
1 large onion
¼ cup oil
3 cloves garlic
¼ cup chopped parsley
*2 cups Boiled Rice**
1½ cups dry white wine

Cut the fish into 4 servings. Salt and pepper them. Melt the butter in a shallow saucepan and fry the fish. Chop the onion and fry it in the oil. Remove from the heat, add crushed garlic and chopped parsley. Add this to the rice, mixing in well, and spread over the fish. Pour over the wine, cover and boil on the low heat for 10 minutes. Remove cover and simmer for another 5–7 minutes. Serve hot. *4 servings*

Sautéed Fish

[Sote iz Treski]

2 pounds fish, such as flounder, pike, halibut
1 teaspoon salt
Dash pepper
½ cup oil
2 onions
2 tablespoons butter
2 cloves garlic, crushed
1½ cups tomato sauce
20 unpitted black olives
½ cup grated cheese
1 tablespoon chopped parsley

Optional: ½ cup flour for fish

Preheat oven to 250° F.

Divide the fish into 8 pieces and salt and pepper them. Heat the oil in the pan and fry fish on both sides. (The fish could be lightly rolled in flour before frying if desired.) Put the fish into oven-proof serving dish and keep hot in oven. Slice the onions and fry in the rest of the oil. Add 2 tablespoons butter. Mix the garlic with the tomato sauce and pour into the onions. Simmer for 3–5 minutes. Arrange the olives round the fish, pour the prepared tomato sauce over fish, sprinkle with cheese, then parsley and serve 2 pieces per person. *4 servings*

Zapekanka *with Salted Herring*

[Zapekanka s Selodkoi]

1 large salted herring
Cold water to cover herring
2 eggs
1 onion
2 cups mashed potato
1 cup torn, soaked in milk and squeezed out white bread
Pepper to taste
1 tablespoon butter
¼ cup bread crumbs
1 egg
½ cup sour cream
¼ cup chopped parsley

Preheat oven to 400° F.

Soak the herring in cold water overnight. Skin and remove all bones. Put through meat grinder or chop very fine. Separate yolks and whites of 2 eggs; chop onion fine. Mix herring with potatoes, bread, onion and egg yolks. Add pepper. Beat the egg whites stiff and fold into mixture. Butter and sprinkle with bread crumbs an oven-proof dish and spread mixture evenly in it, about 2 inches deep. Beat remaining egg and sour cream together and spread over the top. Bake in oven for 20–30 minutes until a golden-brown crust forms on top and bottom. Cut in squares, sprinkle with parsley and serve. *4 servings*

Flounder and Spinach

[Kambala s Shpinatom]

4 fillets boneless flounder
1 teaspoon salt
1 cup dry white wine
2 hard-cooked eggs
2 cups cooked chopped spinach
Dash pepper
1 tablespoon butter
1½ cups milk
1½ tablespoons flour
1 teaspoon lemon juice
¼ cup grated cheese

Preheat oven to 450° F.

Put the fish into a saucepan, salt it lightly and pour the wine over. Bring to a boil, then turn heat off. Chop eggs and mix with spinach. Add remaining salt and pepper and spread in a buttered oven-proof serving dish. Arrange fish fillets on top. Mix milk with flour. Boil up fish stock—the liquid in which the fish was cooked—and add the milk and flour mixture, stirring all the time. Bring it to a boil, remove from the heat and add the lemon juice. Pour the sauce over the fish and spinach, sprinkle with cheese and bake in hot oven for 10 minutes. *4 servings*

MEAT, POULTRY, GAME

(MYASO, PTITZA I DITCH)

Much of Russian cuisine is designed to keep out the cold, and arriving at a Russian house on a winter day you find the kitchen full of hot, delicious smells of traditional warming-up food. You are always greeted as though you have just driven sixty miles through the snow in an open *droshky* and urged to build up your appetite with vodka and *zakuski*. Where other nationalities may be bewailing the weather, the Russians say, "A good *eating* day . . ." rubbing their hands, glancing at the gray sky and streaming windows with satisfaction, hitching their chairs up to the table.

Russians are hearty eaters and often become fat as they get older. Among the simple people this is a matter of pride, an attitude understandable in a country where famine is not unknown.

MEAT DISHES
[Myasniye Bluda]

Zrazi *with Boiled Buckwheat*
[Zrazi s Kashei]

Zrazi are a kind of exuberant Slavic hamburgers which originally came from Poland but are very much loved in Russia. For the best results buy good beef and grind it yourself.

For Zrazi:

2 pounds finely ground beef (it must be ground twice)
1 medium-sized onion, put through grinder with the beef
1 cup torn, soaked in water and squeezed out white bread
1 cup water
1½ teaspoons salt
Pepper

For Filling:

*1½ cups Boiled Buckwheat**
1 cup sliced fried mushrooms
1 small onion, chopped and fried in 1 tablespoon butter
Salt

For Frying:

2 tablespoons butter

For Sauce:

2 cups sour cream

Preheat oven to 350° F.

Mix *zrazi* ingredients thoroughly and divide into 8 parts. Roll into balls on floured board.

Mix together ingredients for filling and divide into 8 parts.

Cut each ball of meat in half and flatten to about ½-inch thickness, like a thin hamburger. Shape the *zrazi* in the depression of a small plate. The meat must be kept moist, so you will need to keep your hands well floured to prevent sticking. Put one-eighth of the filling in the center of one *zrazi* and cover with another *zrazi*. Join the sides together with the help of a knife. Form into round flat shape. Repeat this process till all filling and *zrazi* are used—making 8 *zrazi*.

Heat the butter in a pan and fry the *zrazi* on both sides till brown. Put them side by side in a baking pan or oven-proof dish and bake in a moderate oven for 10 minutes. Pour the sour cream over them and leave in the oven for another 5–10 minutes, till the sauce starts to boil. Take them from the sauce, put on serving dish and pour sauce over. Serve hot. *8 servings*

Pelemeni

Pelemeni probably came from China through the Far Eastern provinces and no doubt descend from Chinese *dim sims*, savory patties, boiled in stock or water. They are now a typical and greatly loved Russian dish. They are a meal in themselves, though often served with soup. They are very like the *gushe barreh* (ravioli soup), sometimes found in Persia, though a different shape.

In the Far East of Russia and in Siberia *pelemeni* are

made in half-moons and are usually eaten with soya sauce, butter, mustard and vinegar. In Central Russia they are made in a half-moon, then curled back and pinched together to look like little shells, and eaten with or without soup, with sour cream, butter, vinegar and mustard.

In Siberia they are made by the hundred and frozen for the hunters, who take bags of them on their trips. Once frozen they will keep for weeks and only need be thrown into boiling water for a few minutes before serving. Siberians believe they taste better after freezing.

During the war, invading foreign soldiers discovered piles of hard-frozen *pelemeni* in the cellar of an abandoned Russian farmhouse. They laboriously chopped them open and finding the meat inside concluded this was a Russian method of storing meat. It was, in fact, only the housewife's supply, kept in case of visitors.

Deep-frozen *pelemeni* are on the market but though they are less trouble they are never quite as good as homemade. Many Russian women still prefer to make their own.

When ready, *pelemeni* are about 1–1¼ inches in diameter and almost round. When served as a complete meal 30–40 should be allowed for each person. They should not be cut, to prevent losing their juice.

To make about 150 *pelemeni:*

For Filling:

1½ pounds finely ground beef
1 medium-sized onion, minced
1 cup water
1½ teaspoons salt
½ teaspoon pepper

For Dough:

3 eggs
2 cups milk
1 teaspoon salt
1½ pounds flour

For Boiling:

7 cups salted water, chicken or beef broth

Mix together ingredients for filling.

Make the dough. Beat eggs, milk, salt together in a mixing bowl, then add flour and mix thoroughly with wooden spoon. Tip onto floured board and knead until springy. The dough should spring back when pressed.

Cut off a section of the dough and roll out to the thickness of less than one-eighth of an inch. Flour it lightly and cut into circles with a glass about 2 inches in diameter.

Put 1 teaspoon of the meat mixture in the center of each circle, fold in half and pinch the edges firmly together; then turn the *pelemeni* and bring together the ends of the semicircle, pinching them to hold them in place. Put it on the floured board. Repeat till all dough and filling are used up.

If *pelemeni* are being made in big quantities for deep-freezing, they must be laid side by side on the floured board as they are made, not touching each other, nor should they touch in the freezer. Once frozen they can be put into plastic bags and kept for weeks.

Bring the water, chicken or beef bouillon to the boil; drop in the *pelemeni,* 50–70 at a time. Lightly stir with a wooden spoon to keep them apart but be careful not to break them. Bring to a boil and boil for 3–4 minutes. When they rise to the top they are cooked. Take them out quickly with a perforated spoon and serve on a hot dish immediately. *4 servings*

Fried Pelemeni
[Zjariniye Pelemeni]

Make *Pelemeni**, cooking in boiling water or bouillon for only 2–3 minutes, then take out and drain. Heat 2 tablespoons butter in a pan and fry *pelemeni* till light brown. Serve hot with mustard. May be eaten as a meal or served as a hot *zakuska.*

V*areniki*

These are rather like *pelemeni* with different fillings which vary in different parts of Russia. There are also Sweet V*areniki**. V*areniki* are always boiled, never fried.

Vareniki, *Peasant Style*
[Vareniki po Derevienski]

For Filling:

1 large onion
1½ tablespoons butter
2 cups mashed potato
½ teaspoon salt
Pepper

For Dough:

*Dough as for Pelemeni**

For Accompaniment:

¾ pound bacon slices
2 large onions, chopped

For Boiling:

4 cups stock or salted water for boiling

Chop 1 onion finely and fry in butter till light brown, then add to mashed potato, with salt and pepper, mixing well. Roll out the dough, cut it out in circles as for *Pelemeni**, put filling in each circle and fold over, leaving in half-moon shapes. Pinch edges together to seal. Put on the floured board. Cut the bacon slices across into small pieces and fry them with 2 chopped onions, till light brown. Pour off excess fat and keep hot.

Boil the stock or salted water and drop in *vareniki.* Cook *vareniki* as for *pelemeni.* Take them from the water and put on a serving dish. Spread the fried bacon and onions on top and serve immediately. *4–6 servings*

Cabbage Rolls

[Golubzi]

Stuffed vegetables and edible leaves, which are also popular in many Middle Eastern countries, probably came to Russia via the Caucasus or through wars with Turkey. In Greece, Turkey and Persia the stuffings are often spiced rice with pine nuts and currants, and yoghurt is eaten as a sauce, but the Caucasians include lamb with rice in their stuffed leaves and replace yoghurt with sour milk mixed with salt, grated garlic, fine sugar and cinnamon.

The Russians prefer sour cream.

When making *golubzi* choose a cabbage that is not too firm; otherwise you will have trouble separating the leaves.

1 medium-sized cabbage
Enough boiling water to cover cabbage

For Filling:

1¼ pounds finely ground beef
*1 cup Boiled Rice**
½ cup chopped onion fried in *1 tablespoon butter*
1½ teaspoons salt
½ teaspoon pepper
2 tablespoons butter for frying
1 cup water or beef stock
1 cup sour cream

Cut off outside leaves and remove core of cabbage head so that the cooking liquid can get to the leaves more easily. Put it upside-down in the saucepan and pour in enough boiling water to fill and cover cabbage. Boil for 10 minutes. Drain off water thoroughly and detach leaves. Trim the thick center vein so that the leaf will fold over easily.

Mix the filling thoroughly, season it and put 1 or 2 tablespoons—depending on the size of the leaves—on the thicker part of a leaf. Fold in 3 sides, then roll it into a parcel. Repeat process till all leaves are filled.

Heat butter in frying pan and fry cabbage rolls lightly. Put them in a saucepan and pour 1 cup water or beef stock over them. Cover, bring to a boil, reduce the heat and simmer for 1 hour, till leaves are tender, if necessary adding more liquid. When cooked pour over the sour cream and simmer for another 5 minutes.

Serve hot in a deep dish, as a complete course. *4 servings*

Boeuf Stroganoff

[Beef Stroganoff]

It is said that a certain Count Stroganoff (more likely his cook), while stationed in the north of Siberia, discovered that his beef was frozen so hard it could only be cut into paper-thin strips. Having sliced it this way the cook added sour cream, thus creating one of the world's great dishes.

We are giving here the original simple recipe as used by

most Russians but there are numerous variations. In South Russia, tomato paste or purée has been introduced; in France, where the dish was quickly recognized as a masterpiece, white wine is used. Different cooks vary the quantity of butter according to how rich they want to make the dish; and green onions are often substituted for onions to give a more delicate flavor. Rump steak is quite suitable but fillet is far better.

2 pounds fillet or rump steak
1 medium-sized onion
1 tablespoon butter
¾ pound mushrooms
1 teaspoon salt
Pepper to taste
½ cup sour cream

Cut the meat into the thinnest possible strips, about ½ inch by 2 inches. This will be easier if it is frozen almost hard. Chop up the onion, fry it in the butter. Slice the mushrooms, add to the onions and fry until almost cooked. Add the meat, salt and pepper and cook for about 10 minutes for fillet steak or 20 minutes for rump. Pour the sour cream over and bring just to the boil. Put in deep dish and serve immediately.

Boeuf Stroganoff is usually eaten with French-fried potatoes or plain boiled rice. Green vegetables or green salad are also good accompaniments. *4 servings*

Meat Rolls

[Myasniye Roliki]

2 pounds thin rump steak
1 teaspoon salt
½ teaspoon pepper
½ pound sliced bacon
2 carrots, peeled and sliced lengthwise
1 parsnip, peeled and sliced lengthwise
1 onion, sliced
1 tablespoon butter
1 tablespoon flour
1½ cups stock or water
½ cup tomato sauce

Garniture:

*Salted Cucumber**
*Marinaded Beets**

Pound the meat lightly, until it is about ¼ inch thick, then cut it into pieces about 3 inches by 5 inches. Sprinkle with salt and pepper. On each piece put 1 slice of bacon, 1 slice of carrot, of parsnip, and of onion. Roll up tightly and fasten with a toothpick. Fry in butter till brown, sprinkle with flour and put into a saucepan. Swill out frying pan with 1 cup of stock or water, pour it over the rolls, add the tomato sauce and the rest of the vegetables not used in the rolls. Simmer, covered, for 1 hour, till tender. Remove toothpicks, put in a deep serving dish and pour sauce over. Garnish with Salted Cucumber* and Marinaded Beets*.

This dish is usually eaten with boiled rice. *4 servings*

Beef Stew

[Gulyash]

1½–2 pounds beef steak
1 tablespoon butter or fat for frying
1–2 cups hot bouillon or water
1 cup tomato purée
1 bay leaf
1½ teaspoons salt
Pepper to taste
1 cup chopped onion
1 tablespoon fat or butter

Garniture:

¼ cup chopped dill or parsley

Cut the meat into 1-inch dice and fry it in the butter or fat until light brown. Pour the hot bouillon or water over it and add half the cup of tomato purée, the bay leaf, salt and pepper. Simmer, covered, 1–1½ hours.

Fry the onion in fat or butter and add the rest of the tomato purée, with more bouillon if needed. Add to meat and simmer again for 15 minutes. Serve with boiled potatoes sprinkled with dill or parsley.

This recipe can be used for pork, with lard instead of butter for frying, and half the quantity of tomato purée. Simply fry the pork and onions together, sprinkle with flour, then add the rest of the ingredients and cook till tender. *4 servings*

Pot Roast with Macaroni

[Tushonoe Myaso s Macaronami]

Salt
Pepper
2–2½ pounds tip or rump steak in one piece
1 tablespoon fat or butter for frying
2 cups hot water
2 medium-sized onions
2 bay leaves
½ teaspoon peppercorns
½ cup fresh or sour cream
½ pound macaroni
1 tablespoon salt
8 cups boiling water
1 tablespoon butter

Rub the salt and pepper into the meat and fry in fat or butter till brown all over. Put it into a saucepan, swill out the frying pan with 2 cups hot water and pour over the meat. Coarsely chop the onions, and add to the meat with bay leaves and peppercorns. Cook on low heat for 1–1½ hours. The meat must be tender but not over-cooked. Add sour cream to the gravy. Put the macaroni into 8 cups fast-boiling salted water, bring to boil again, turn down heat and boil on low heat till tender, about 15 minutes. Strain off water and add butter to macaroni. Cut the meat into slices, arrange on a dish and garnish with the macaroni. Serve immediately.

This pot roast is very good cold. *6 servings*

Kotletki

Russians love *kotletki* almost as much as *Pelemeni** and Salted Cucumber*, and eat them constantly. They are extremely good and very easy for a snack, being made of ground meat, like hamburgers. They are no relation to the French *côtelette* or the English cutlet.

Pork Kotletki

[Kotletki iz Svinini]

2 pounds finely ground pork, without too much fat
1 cup torn, soaked in water and squeezed out white bread
1 egg
1 cup water
1½ teaspoons salt
Pepper
1 cup bread crumbs
2 tablespoons butter

Put all the ingredients, except the bread crumbs and butter, into a bowl and mix them thoroughly with a wooden spoon. Form into oblong-shaped cakes, using about 1 heaped tablespoon of mixture for each.

Roll them in bread crumbs, flatten them with the blade of a knife to about ½ inch thickness and fry in butter for 10–15 minutes, until the meat is cooked. Serve with Boiled Buckwheat* or French-fried or mashed potatoes and green vegetables. *6 servings*

Beef Kotletki
[Kotletki iz Govyadini]

2 pounds finely ground beef
1 cup torn, soaked in water and squeezed out white bread
1 egg
1 cup water
½ teaspoon salt
¼ teaspoon pepper
1 cup bread crumbs
2 tablespoons butter
1 tablespoon flour
1 cup water

Mix together the beef, bread, egg, water, salt and pepper. Form into *kotletki*, roll in bread crumbs and fry in butter. Keep hot and make sauce by adding the flour to the butter and juice in the pan.

Brown the mixture, then add 1 cup of water, stirring continually. Serve the sauce in a sauceboat, not poured over the *kotletki*. This dish is usually accompanied by mashed potato, buttered carrots and Salted Cucumber*. *6 servings*

Stewed Lamb with Cabbage
[Tuschonka]

2 pounds lamb leg chops or steak
1 teaspoon salt
2 tablespoons butter
1 small cabbage
½ cup chopped onion
½ pound sauerkraut
Pepper to taste
1 bay leaf
1 cup hot water

Garniture:

Dill or parsley

Wash and remove the fat from the meat and cut the meat into 1-inch dice. Salt meat and brown in butter. Put in a casserole or saucepan.

Shred the cabbage into ½-inch strips. Fry the onion in butter steak was fried in, add the cabbage and fry lightly together. Add the sauerkraut, pepper, bay leaf and hot water. Mix all in with the meat and bring to a boil. Simmer, covered, for 1½ hours, until meat is tender. Arrange in a deep dish, garnish with dill or parsley, and serve with boiled potatoes.

The same recipe can be used with pork instead of lamb.
4 servings

Stewed Cabbage with Bacon and Frankfurters

[Tuschonka s Sosiskami]

1 small cabbage
½ cup chopped onions
2 tablespoons butter
½ teaspoon salt
Pepper to taste
1 bay leaf
1 cup hot water
½ pound bacon
1 pound frankfurters

Garniture:

Dill or parsley

Shred the cabbage into ½-inch strips and fry it with the chopped onions in butter. Add the salt, pepper, bay leaf and hot water, bring to boil and simmer, covered, for 1 hour. Cut the bacon and frankfurters into small pieces and fry lightly. Add to the cabbage and cook for another half hour. Serve with boiled potatoes sprinkled with dill or parsley.
4 servings

Tongue with Vegetables

[Yazik s Ovoschami]

2 pounds fresh tongue—sheep, ox or pork
Enough cold salted water to cover tongue
½ pound bacon
1 cup ½-inch diced carrots
1 cup ½-inch diced rutabaga
1 cup chopped cabbage or Brussels sprouts
1 cup chopped onion
½ cup chopped parsley
1 teaspoon salt
Pepper to taste
1 bay leaf
1½ cups bouillon
1½ cups diced potatoes
*2½ cups White Sauce**

Garniture:

Parsley or dill

Put the tongue into a saucepan, cover with cold salted water and bring to a boil. Reduce the heat and simmer until tender. When cool, take off the skin and cut the tongue into 1-inch dice. Cut up the bacon and mix together bacon, tongue and all the vegetables except the potatoes. Add the parsley, salt, pepper and bay leaf. Add the bouillon, bring to a boil and simmer for 20 minutes. Add potatoes and simmer until well done, about another 15 minutes.

Add the white sauce. Stir it in gently, bring to a boil, and remove from heat. Serve in a deep dish, sprinkled with parsley or dill. *6 servings*

Tongue in Bread Crumbs

[Yazik v Suharyach]

1 ox tongue
Enough cold salted water to cover tongue
1 egg
1 cup bread crumbs
2 tablespoons butter

Put the tongue in a saucepan of cold salted water, bring to a boil, reduce heat and simmer until tender. Cool it and remove the skin. Cut it in slices ½ inch thick. Just before serving, dip slices in beaten egg, roll in bread crumbs and quickly fry in hot butter. *3 servings*

Meat or Vegetable Rolls

[Ruleti]

These are rolls of ground meat or mashed potato, with various fillings.

Meat Roll with Vegetables

[Myasnoi Rulet s Ovoschami]

For the Roll:

2 pounds beef that has been ground twice
1 medium-sized onion, minced
1 cup torn, soaked in water and squeezed out white bread
1 cup water
1½ teaspoons salt
Pepper to taste

For Filling:

1 cup diced cooked carrot
½ pound cooked green peas
1 medium-sized onion, chopped and fried in 1 tablespoon butter
Butter to grease pan
1 egg
¼ cup bread crumbs

For Gravy:

1 tablespoon flour
½ cup water

Preheat oven to 350° F.

Mix together the beef, minced onion, bread, water, salt and pepper. Spread out, about ¾ inch thick, on a wet cloth or sheet of plastic.

Arrange the cooked vegetables for the filling down the center of the meat. Carefully fold the meat over them to make a roll, joining the edges together. Gently slide it from the cloth or plastic sheet onto a buttered roasting pan with the joined side underneath. Smear the top with beaten egg, sprinkle with bread crumbs and bake in a moderate oven for 1–1½ hours. Put on a serving dish and keep warm. Make a gravy by thickening pan juice with the flour mixed with water. Bring to a boil, stirring all the time. Serve gravy separately. This dish is usually eaten with mashed or French-fried potatoes, which could be arranged along one side of the roll. 6 *servings*

Meat Roll with Boiled Buckwheat and Mushrooms
[Myasnoi Rulet s Kashei i Gribami]

The ingredients for the roll are exactly the same as listed for Meat Roll with Vegetables*.

For Filling:

1 small onion, chopped
½ pound sliced mushrooms
1 tablespoon butter
*1½ cups Boiled Buckwheat**
½ teaspoon salt
Butter to grease pan

For Sauce:

1 cup sour cream

Preheat oven to 350° F.

Mix the ingredients for the roll together and spread on a wet cloth or plastic sheet.

To make the filling, fry onion and mushrooms in butter, add to boiled buckwheat, with salt to taste, and arrange mixture down the center of the meat. Fold meat over to make a roll, slide from cloth or plastic sheet into a well-buttered roasting pan, joined side down, and bake in a moderate oven for 1–1½ hours. Pour the sour cream over and serve as a complete course with buttered carrots or peas. *6 servings*

Alternative Fillings for Meat Roll

Egg and Green Onion Filling

[Yaitza s Lukom]

6 hard-cooked eggs
1 bunch green onions lightly fried in 1 tablespoon butter
¼ teaspoon salt
Pepper to taste

Make the roll as for Meat Roll with Vegetables*. Chop up the eggs and mix with onions. Add salt and pepper. Arrange down the center of the roll, seal and bake as in Meat Roll with Vegetables*.

Mushroom and Onion Filling

[Myasnoi Rulet s Gribami i Lukom]

1 large onion
1½ pounds mushrooms
¼ teaspoon salt
Pepper to taste
1 tablespoon butter

Make roll as for Meat Roll with Vegetables*. Chop up onion and mushrooms, add salt and pepper and fry in butter. Arrange down center of roll and bake in oven as in Meat Roll with Vegetables*.

Mashed Potato Roll with Meat Filling

[Kartofelnii Rulet s Myasom]

1½ pounds potatoes
1 teaspoon salt
1½ tablespoons butter
½ cup milk
½ cup flour
2 eggs

For Filling:

½ cup chopped onion
1½ tablespoons butter for frying onion
1 pound finely ground meat
1 teaspoon salt
Pepper to taste
1 tablespoon flour
Butter to grease pan
1 tablespoon fine bread crumbs
2 tablespoons melted butter for basting

Preheat oven to 350° F.

Peel, boil and drain the potatoes. Mash them well, adding 1 teaspoon salt, 1½ tablespoons butter and the milk. Soften butter and heat milk before adding. (An electric mixer or blender makes excellent smooth mashed potato.) Cool for 5–

10 minutes, then add ½ cup flour and the beaten eggs, reserving a little of the egg for later.

Fry the onion in butter, add the meat and 1 teaspoon salt and the pepper. When almost cooked sprinkle in 1 tablespoon flour, stirring continually. Cool for a few minutes.

On a well-floured board or cloth, spread out the mashed potato mixture, making it about ½ inch thickness. Spread the cooked meat filling over one half, to about an inch from the edge. Fold over the other half and join the edges. Slide onto a buttered roasting pan, form it into the shape of a loaf, smear with beaten egg and sprinkle with bread crumbs. Bake in a moderate oven for 30 minutes, until golden brown, basting occasionally with butter.

Serve with carrots and peas in White Sauce*. *6 servings*

As with Meat Roll the fillings could be varied; for instance:

Egg and Mushroom Filling

1 tablespoon butter
½ pound sliced mushrooms
1 onion, chopped
3–4 hard-cooked eggs, chopped

For Sauce:

1 cup sour cream

Preheat oven to 350° F.

Melt the butter in frying pan, add mushrooms and onion and fry together till soft. Mix well with eggs, spread on mashed potato (prepared as for Mashed Potato Roll*) which you have spread out on floured board or cloth. Roll up and bake as for Mashed Potato Roll with Meat Filling*.

When browned, pour 1 cup sour cream over and leave in oven a few minutes longer.

Plain Potato Roll

[Kartofelnii Rulet]

This may be served as accompaniment to meat or fish.

2 pounds potatoes
¾ teaspoon salt
½ cup warmed milk
1 tablespoon melted butter
½ cup chopped onion
1½ tablespoons butter for cooking
Butter to grease pan

Preheat oven to 350° F.

Peel, boil and drain the potatoes and mash well. Add salt, warmed milk and 1 tablespoon melted butter. Fry onion in butter and mix into the potato. Have ready a well-buttered roasting pan and put the potato in, shaping it into a roll in the pan to avoid breaking. Bake in a moderate oven about 30 minutes, till golden brown. *6 servings*

Meat and Vegetable Stew

[Azu]

1½ pounds tip or rump steak
½ teaspoon salt
Pepper
2 tablespoons fat or butter
2 medium-sized onions
1½ cups bouillon or hot water
½ cup tomato sauce
2 tomatoes
1 tablespoon flour
*1 Salted Cucumber**
2–3 cloves garlic
1½ pounds potatoes, French-fried

Cut the meat into ½-inch-wide strips, add salt and pepper and fry in fat or butter till light brown. Chop onions, add to meat and fry lightly. Add 1 cup bouillon or hot water, tomato sauce, tomatoes, skinned and coarsely chopped. Simmer, covered, till the meat is tender, about 30 minutes.

Drain meat juice into another saucepan, add ½ cup bouillon, thicken carefully with flour and bring to a boil. Add the cucumber cut in slices and the garlic, which you have crushed.

Put the French-fried potatoes on the meat, pour the sauce over and simmer for 5–10 minutes. Serve as a complete course with buttered vegetables or Marinaded Beets*. *6 servings*

Beef and Herring

[Forshmack]

1½ pounds boiled beef
1 salted herring, skinned and boned
1½ cups boiled potatoes
1 medium onion
½ cup sour cream
2 eggs
Salt to taste
Pepper to taste
1 tablespoon butter
1 tablespoon bread crumbs
1 tablespoon grated cheese

Preheat oven to 350° F.

Put the meat, herring, potatoes and onion through the grinder. Mix them together thoroughly; add the sour cream, all but 1 tablespoonful. Separate the egg yolks and whites and add the yolks, with the salt and pepper to the meat mixture. Mix again. Beat whites of eggs till stiff and fold in carefully.

Butter small individual oven-proof dishes, or one large dish. Spoon in the mixture, sprinkle with bread crumbs and cheese and bake in a moderate oven for approximately 15 minutes, until *Forshmack* is heated through. Pour 1 tablespoon sour cream over the top and serve hot. *4 servings*

A popular and typical variation of this dish is Beef and Herring in Bread Crust (*Forshmack v Kalache*). It is traditionally made in a large horseshoe loaf (*kalach*) but a long French loaf could be used instead.

Take out the center of the loaf, sprinkle the cleaned-out crust with milk and fill it with the Beef and Herring* mixture.

Brush crust with melted butter, sprinkle with grated cheese and bake in a moderate oven, 350°–400° F., for 10 minutes.

If this is served as a hot *zakuska* it should be cut in slices before it is brought to the table. If it is eaten as a separate course it should be accompanied by a White Sauce*. When cold it is excellent picnic food.

Stew

[Ragu]

Ragu is very popular in all Russian households. There are about twelve variations, using lamb, pork, oxtail, hare or rabbit, chicken, veal, giblets, tongue, etc. All kinds of vegetables may be included and it may be served with different garnishes.

This recipe for *Ragu* of Tongue can also be used for lamb, pork, oxtail, veal or rabbit.

1½–2 pounds tongue
Cold water to cover tongue
1 onion
2 carrots, peeled
1 rutabaga, peeled
1 parsnip, peeled
3 potatoes
3 tablespoons fat or butter
1 teaspoon salt
Pepper to taste
1 bay leaf
½ cup tomato sauce
1 cup bouillon

Garniture:

Dill or parsley

Boil the tongue until tender, then cool, peel off the skin and cut meat into dice.

Peel, wash and dice all the vegetables and fry them lightly in the fat or butter. Put them into a casserole with the tongue, then salt, pepper and bay leaf, tomato sauce and bouillon. Simmer, covered, for 30–35 minutes, until all vegetables are cooked. Serve in a deep dish sprinkled with dill or parsley. *6 servings*

Pork Fillets with Apple

[Sviniye Odbivniye s Yablockami]

1½ pounds pork tenderloin or chops
½ teaspoon salt
1 tablespoon lard or fat
1 large onion
3 large cooking apples
½ cup stock or water

Remove all sinews and unwanted fat from the meat, pound it lightly, salt it and fry in fat on both sides. Slice the onion, add and fry together. Peel and slice the apples. When onions are light brown add the apples and stock or water. Cover and simmer for 15 minutes. Serve with Boiled Rice* or potatoes. *3 servings*

Suckling Pig with Boiled Buckwheat

[Porosyonok s Kashei]

1 suckling pig weighing 8–10 pounds
1 tablespoon salt
1 cup sour cream
6 small apples
Little water
½ cup melted lard
*1 pound Boiled Buckwheat**
4 hard-cooked eggs
*Horseradish Sauce**

Preheat oven to 350° F.

Rub the pig with salt, inside and out; smear all over with sour cream. Fill with unpeeled apples, whole or halved. Put the pig in the roasting pan, belly down, with a little water and some lard. Bake in a moderate oven. Every 15–20 minutes smear it with fresh melted lard. Do not use the pan juice for basting. If the pig's back is browning too fast cover it with brown paper or foil until sides are the same color. Test to see if it is done by piercing the thickest part of the back leg. If the meat juice is not red the meat is cooked. The average time is 1½–2 hours.

When cooked, move pig to another pan and keep hot. Put the boiled buckwheat into the roasting pan you used for the pig and mix it with the meat juice. Chop up two of the hard-cooked eggs and add to buckwheat. Put the buckwheat on a large dish, lay the suckling pig on it, and decorate with some of the cooked apples and the remaining two hard-cooked eggs cut in long sections.

If you prefer, the pig could be carved in the kitchen and arranged on the buckwheat before coming to the table. The horseradish sauce is served separately.

If this dish is too rich, pour off some of the fat before putting the buckwheat into the roasting pan. *10–12 servings*

Ham Cooked in Beer

[Boujenina]

This is a very ancient Russian recipe, often mentioned in the accounts of early travelers and still popular.

1 teaspoon salt
4–5 pounds of the center part of a leg of pork
¼ pound bacon or ham fat, cut into strips
1 tablespoon fat for cooking
1½ cups beer

Preheat oven to 400° F.

Salt the meat all over. With a long sharp knife pierce it through in several places and insert the strips of bacon or ham fat. Put the meat with the fat into a roasting pan. Put into the heated oven and when it starts to roast pour half the beer over it. Repeat with the rest of the beer in 30 minutes. Baste with combined beer and pan juice every 15–20 minutes. Bake for 1½ hours. Serve with stewed cabbage and boiled potatoes. *8 servings*

Veal Steak with Pork Filling

[Schnitzel so Svinim Farshom]

4 veal steaks cut from the leg, about 6 by 6 inches and ½ inch thick
½ teaspoon salt
Pepper to taste

For Filling:

1 pound lean pork
¼ pound ham
½ pound button mushrooms
1 tablespoon butter
½ teaspoon nutmeg
½ cup milk
½ teaspoon salt
2 tablespoons butter for frying

For Sauce:

½ cup chopped onion
½ cup tomato purée
1 cup water

Pound the steaks lightly and sprinkle with salt and pepper. To make filling: mince the pork, chop the ham fine; slice the mushrooms and fry them in butter. Mix together all ingredients for filling. Divide into four and put one part in the center of each veal fillet, arranging filling lengthwise. Roll the veal round the filling and tie in two or three places with thin string or use toothpicks. Heat butter in the frying pan and fry the veal rolls, browning them all over; then put them in a saucepan. Fry the onion in the rest of the butter, in frying pan, and add the tomato purée and water. Bring to a boil and pour over the rolls in the saucepan. Cover, and simmer for 30 minutes. Arrange the rolls on a long dish and either pour the sauce over them or serve separately.

This dish looks and tastes good with grilled tomato halves, green beans and Boiled Rice*. *4 servings*

Boiled Beef Pudding

[Puding iz Varyonogo Myasa]

2½ pounds boneless chuck steak
1½ teaspoons salt
Enough cold water to cover meat
1 large onion
Pepper
1 cup torn, soaked in milk and squeezed out white bread
2 eggs
Butter to grease bowl

Garniture:

¼ cup chopped parsley or dill

Put the meat and salt into cold water, bring to a boil, then reduce heat and simmer for 1½ hours. Leave to cool in liquid; then put beef and the onion through the meat grinder, twice, adding the pepper. Add bread. Separate egg yolks and whites and add the yolks. Mix all well together. Beat the egg whites stiff and fold into the meat mixture. Put into a greased 8-cup pudding basin, cover with lid and stand three-quarters submerged in a saucepan of water. Cook on low heat for 40–50 minutes. Turn out onto dish and sprinkle with parsley or dill. *4 servings*

POULTRY
[Ptitza]

Preparation of Poultry and Game for Chicken à la Kiev *and* Kotletki

To fillet chicken, turkey, duck, woodcock, partridge or pheasant: lay the bird on its back. Remove skin from breast and with a very sharp knife cut out the white meat, including the top section of the wing, with the bone, as far down as the first joint. Lift out small fillet carefully. Remove any sinews and pound the fillet to about ¼ inch thickness. If filleting chicken for à la Kiev be careful not to separate the meat from the wing bone; otherwise the bone is removed.

If you have an obliging butcher you may be able to persuade him to do this for you.

Chicken à la Kiev
[Kievskiye Kotletki]

½ cup butter, very *cold*
4 fillets chicken, with wing bone
½ teaspoon salt
2 eggs
¼ cup milk
1½ cups bread crumbs
2–3 cups chicken fat or vegetable oil for deep-frying

Cut the butter into strips about 3 inches long and ½ inch thick. Put it in the refrigerator. It must be kept absolutely cold and hard until the moment of using.

Sprinkle the Kiev fillets with salt, lay them on the table, pound lightly and in the center of each put a strip of cold butter. Roll the flesh round the butter, leaving the wing bone projecting like the stalk of a pear. Be sure the butter is completely sealed inside the fillet. Dip into eggs beaten with milk, roll in bread crumbs, dip in egg again and roll again in crumbs. Deep-fry in hot fat for 4 or 5 minutes. The fillets must be served immediately they are ready. French-fried or mashed potatoes, green peas, carrots or cauliflower dusted with fried bread crumbs are good accompaniments for this dish. *4 servings*

Chicken Fillets in Bread Crumbs

[Fille Zeplyonka v Suharyach]

This is a very much simpler preparation than Kiev Chicken.

4 fillets cut from the chicken without the wing bone (see Preparation of Poultry and Game for Chicken à la Kiev*)
½ teaspoon salt
1 egg
1 cup bread crumbs
¼ pound butter or ½ cup oil for frying

Sprinkle the fillets with salt, dip them into the beaten egg and roll in bread crumbs. Melt the butter or oil in preheated skillet and fry fillets for 5–7 minutes. Serve immediately with French-fried potatoes, green peas, young buttered carrots or cauliflower dusted with fried bread crumbs. *4 servings*

Chicken and Mushrooms in Sour-cream Sauce

[Zeplyonok s Gribami v Smetaniye]

1 chicken weighing about 2½ pounds
1½ teaspoons salt
Enough cold water to cover chicken
1 pound mushrooms
1½ tablespoons butter
1 cup sour cream

Put the chicken with the salt into cold water, bring to a boil, turn down heat and simmer until tender, about 40 minutes. When cool cut it into pieces, removing all bones and skin. Coarsely slice the mushrooms and lightly fry in butter. Add sour cream. Add the chicken and mix together. Remove from the heat and let it stand on the stove in a warm place for 5 minutes, keeping hot but not cooking. Serve with Boiled Rice* or mashed potatoes. *4 servings*

Boiled Fowl Fried in Bread Crumbs

[Kuritza v Suharyach]

1 stewing fowl, about 3 pounds
Enough cold water to cover fowl
1 tablespoon salt
3 carrots, peeled
1 onion
2 eggs
½ cup milk
2 cups bread crumbs
4 tablespoons butter for frying

Put the fowl in cold water with the salt, carrots and onion, bring to a boil, reduce heat and simmer for 2–2½ hours. Lcavc it to cool in its stock, which makes it juicier. When cold, take it out, cut it in pieces, dip it in beaten egg mixed with milk and roll in bread crumbs. Fry quickly in butter. Serve with French-fried potatoes and the re-warmed carrots cooked with the fowl.

This can be served as a *zakuska* and eaten hot or cold. *6 servings*

Fowl with Rice and White Sauce

[Kuritza s Risom i Bielim Sousom]

1 stewing fowl
Enough cold water to cover fowl
1 tablespoon salt
3 carrots
1 onion

For Sauce:

2 tablespoons plain flour
½ cup water
2 tablespoons sour cream
Juice ½ lemon
*6 cups hot Boiled Rice**

Put the fowl in cold water with the salt, carrots and onion, bring to boil, then simmer for 2–2½ hours. Keep hot in the stock. Take 2 cups of this chicken stock and put into a separate saucepan and bring to a boil. Mix together the flour and ½ cup of water, pour it into the stock, stirring all the time, and add the sour cream. Bring just up to a boil. Add lemon juice. Arrange the hot boiled rice on a dish and set the pieces of fowl round it. The sauce is served separately or poured over all. *6 servings*

Chahohbili *of Chicken*

[Chahohbili]

This Caucasian dish comes from Georgia but is very popular in all parts of Russia.

1 chicken, weighing about 2–2½ pounds
2 tablespoons butter
1 large onion, chopped
1 teaspoon salt
Pepper to taste
1 bay leaf
½ cup tomato sauce
1 cup chicken stock
Juice ½ lemon
2–3 medium-sized tomatoes
1 tablespoon butter for frying tomatoes

Disjoint the chicken and fry it in 2 tablespoons butter. Add the onion and fry together till golden brown. Put into a casserole with salt, pepper, bay leaf, tomato sauce and stock. Simmer, covered, for 20–30 minutes. Add the lemon juice. Skin the tomatoes, cut in halves and fry in 1 tablespoon butter. Put the *Chahohbili* into a deep dish, arrange the tomatoes on top and serve with Boiled Rice*. *4 servings*

Poultry Ragu

[Ragu iz Kuritzi]

1 chicken, about 2½–3 pounds weight
2 tablespoons butter for frying
2 apples
2 carrots, peeled
1 onion
½ pound mushrooms
1 parsnip, peeled
2 potatoes
½ pound green peas
½ cup golden raisins
1½ teaspoons salt
1 cup bouillon

Cut the chicken into pieces and lightly fry in butter. Take from frying pan and put into a casserole. Peel, wash and cut apples and all vegetables, except peas, into small dice. Fry lightly in the melted butter you used for the chicken. Put fried apples and vegetables into the casserole with the chicken, add peas, raisins, salt and bouillon. Cover and simmer for 30 minutes, till all is cooked. Serve with fried or boiled potatoes or Boiled Rice*.

The same recipe can be used for stewing fowl, goose, duck, giblets or a combination of all these. If using stewing fowl it should be cooked for 1 hour before frying. *6 servings*

Poultry Kotletki

[Kuriniye Kotletki]

1½ pounds chicken or fowl fillets
1 cup torn, soaked in milk and squeezed out white bread
1 tablespoon butter
1 teaspoon salt
1 egg
½ cup bread crumbs
3 tablespoons butter for frying

Skin and remove all sinews from the fillets. Put fillets through the meat grinder 3 times. Add the squeezed-out bread, 1 tablespoon butter and salt. Mix all together thoroughly, form into oblong *kotletki* about 3½ inches long and ½ inch thick. Dip in beaten egg, roll in bread crumbs and fry in butter. Serve with buttered carrots, green peas and fried potatoes. *3 servings*

Chicken Kotletki *with Mushroom Filling in Sour Cream*

[Kotletki iz Zeplyonka s Gribami v Smetanei]

½ pound mushrooms
1 tablespoon butter
1½ pounds chicken fillets
1 cup torn, soaked in milk and squeezed out white bread
1 tablespoon softened butter
1 teaspoon salt
1 egg
1 cup fine bread crumbs
2 tablespoons butter for frying
1 cup sour cream

Chop mushrooms and fry in butter. Put chicken through meat grinder, add bread, butter and salt, combining well together. Make into oblong *kotletki*, using about 1 heaped tablespoon for each. Flatten each one slightly and in the center put the fried mushroom filling; then fold over, patting with hands. Seal by dipping in beaten egg, roll in bread crumbs and fry in butter. When cooked, pour sour cream over the *kotletki* and simmer in pan for 3 minutes. Serve with Boiled Rice*.

Variations of fillings could include chopped egg and green onions, or chestnut purée. *3 servings*

Roast Turkey with Chestnuts and Apples

[Indyushka s Kaschtanami i Yablokami]

1 turkey, weighing about 8 pounds
1 tablespoon salt

For Filling:

1½ cups canned apple
3 cups unsweetened canned chestnut purée
2 tablespoons butter or fat for roasting

For Gravy:

½ cup bouillon
1 tablespoon flour

Preheat oven to 400° F.

Prepare the turkey for roasting and rub it with salt inside and out. Mash together the apple and chestnut purée and stuff the turkey. Sew up the opening and roast in butter or poultry fat, basting occasionally. The roasting time will vary with the size of the turkey but an 8-pound bird takes about 2–2½ hours. A larger bird will take longer. Test for readiness by piercing the thickest part of the leg. If the juice that comes out is not red and the meat is tender the bird is ready.

Keep the turkey hot on a large dish and make the gravy by adding the bouillon and flour to the liquid in the roasting pan, after straining off excess fat. Serve with Boiled Buckwheat*, French-fried potatoes, green peas and buttered carrots. *8–10 servings*

If canned chestnut purée is not available or if fresh chestnuts are preferred, make the stuffing the following way:

Fresh Chestnut Stuffing

Enough chestnuts to fill the bird when mixed with apples
Boiling water for blanching
1 cup milk
4 medium-sized apples
½ cup water
2 tablespoons butter
Pinch salt

Blanch the chestnuts with boiling water and take off the skins. Put them in a saucepan with the milk. Boil, covered, for 20–30 minutes. Peel, cut up and cook the apples on low heat, with ½ cup water, till soft. Put the chestnuts and apples through meat grinder, or mash them together, adding the butter and salt. Stuff the turkey, sew up and roast. *8–10 servings*

Roast Turkey with Liver Filling

[Indyushka s Petchonkoi]

1 turkey, about 8 pounds weight
1 tablespoon salt

For Filling:

2 eggs
1 pound calf liver
3 tablespoons butter
1 cup torn, soaked in milk and squeezed out white bread
1 teaspoon salt
Pepper to taste
2 tablespoons butter or poultry fat for roasting

For Gravy:

1 tablespoon flour
½ cup bouillon

Preheat oven to 400° F.

Prepare the turkey for roasting and rub with salt inside and out. To make filling: separate the egg yolks and whites. Cut the liver into pieces, removing all sinews. Fry lightly in 1 tablespoon butter, then put through the meat grinder twice with 2 tablespoons butter and the squeezed out bread. Add salt, pepper and the egg yolks. Mix well. Beat the egg whites stiffly and blend in carefully with the liver mixture.

Put this stuffing into the bird and sew up the opening. Do not pack the stuffing in too tightly, it swells in cooking. Put the turkey into the oven with 2 tablespoons butter or poultry fat spread on it and baste about every 15–20 minutes. Cook approximately 2–2½ hours. When cooked keep the turkey hot on a dish while making the gravy. Add the flour and bouillon to the pan juice, and boil it up to thicken. *8 servings*

Roast Duck with Apples

[Utka s Yablockami]

1 duck, 5 pounds weight
1 tablespoon salt
6 small apples
2 tablespoons butter or poultry fat for cooking
1 pound potatoes
1 pound sweet potatoes
1 cup bouillon or water
1 tablespoon sour cream

Preheat oven to 400° F.

Prepare the duck for roasting. Rub it with salt inside and out. Wash the apples and cut them in halves. Fill the duck with apples and sew it up. Put in the roasting pan and spread with butter or fat. Roast for 30 minutes. Add the peeled potatoes and sweet potatoes and roast all together, basting occasionally for another 1–1½ hours.

When cooked, put the duck on a dish with apples on one side and potatoes on the other. Keep hot while you make the gravy by adding the bouillon and sour cream to the pan juice. Serve gravy in a sauceboat.

This recipe could also be used with goose. *6 servings*

Duck with Stewed Cabbage

[Utka s Kapustoi]

1 duck, about 4 pounds weight	*2 cups bouillon or water*
1 teaspoon salt	*1 small cabbage*
3 tablespoons butter for frying	*1 small onion*
	2 apples
	½ teaspoon salt

Cut the duck into large pieces, salt it and fry in butter till golden brown. Put in a deep casserole with a lid, add a little of the bouillon or water, cover and simmer for 30 minutes.

Cut up the cabbage and onion and fry lightly in butter the duck was fried in. Peel and slice the apples and add, with ½ teaspoon salt and the rest of the bouillon. Simmer till the cabbage is tender, about 30 minutes. Mix in with the duck and cook on low heat for another 30 minutes. Serve with boiled potatoes or Boiled Rice*. *4 servings*

Goose with Noodles

[Goos s Lapschoi]

1½–2 pounds goose, cut in pieces	*1 cup bouillon or water*
3 tablespoons butter	*½ pound egg noodles*
1 teaspoon salt	*1 teaspoon salt for noodles*
	4 cups water to boil noodles

Garniture:

Dill or parsley

Brown the pieces of goose in butter, then add salt and bouillon and simmer in covered saucepan until the meat is cooked, approximately 1 hour. Put the noodles in boiling salted water, boil for 10 minutes, drain off, put them on top of the goose meat and simmer for 5–10 minutes. Arrange all in a deep dish, sprinkle with dill or parsley and serve as a complete course. *4 servings*

GAME

[Ditch]

Russia has a wonderful variety of game which can be used for the table . . . wild duck, partridge, grouse, woodcock, hazel hen, capercailzie, hare, deer and even bear. Those who have eaten both say that cured and smoked haunch of wild bear from Southern Russia is excellent but Siberian bears are tough.

In the old days bears were trapped by putting a copper jar with a narrow neck, baited with honey, near a den. The bear pushed his muzzle in to lick the honey and could not get his head out again.

Pheasant

[Faizan]

1 pheasant
3 tablespoons butter
1 pound button mushrooms
½ pound small onions
1 teaspoon salt
1 cup bouillon

Fry the pheasant in butter till golden brown all over, then remove into a deep casserole. Lightly fry the mushrooms and onions in butter used for pheasant, and spread them over the bird. Add salt and bouillon and simmer, covered, until cooked, about 45 minutes. *4 servings*

Pheasant with Mushrooms in Sour-cream Sauce

[Faizan s Gribami v Smetaniye]

1 pheasant
2 tablespoons butter
1 pound button mushrooms
½ cup bouillon
1 teaspoon salt
1 cup sour cream

Cut the pheasant into pieces and fry them lightly in butter. Add the mushrooms, bouillon and salt. Simmer for 30 minutes. Add the sour cream, bring to a boil and simmer for 15 minutes. Serve with Boiled Rice* or French-fried potatoes. *4 servings*

Game Birds Cooked in Clay

This method is suitable for quail, plover, snipe, and is used by huntsmen.

Draw the birds, fill them with butter and salt, cover in clay and put in the fire. When the clay cracks the birds are ready. The feathers come off with the clay.

Preparation of Deer, Wild Pig, Bear, Goat, Hare

[Prigotavlieniye Ditchi]

To remove the strong flavor from the meat of wild animals, cut the meat from loin and hind legs into pieces weighing about 2–3 pounds and soak them in cold water for 3–4 hours. Then put into cold Marinade for Game* for 3 or 4 days, keeping it in the refrigerator.

Hare needs only 24 hours in the marinade and need not be cut up. The whole animal can be cooked.

Marinade for Game

[Marinad dla Ditchi]

7 cups water
1¼ ounces acetic acid, 33.33 strength
1 tablespoon salt
1 tablespoon sugar
2–3 bay leaves
1 teaspoon peppercorns
1 onion
1 branch parsley

Boil all the ingredients together for 10 minutes. Cool. Pour the mixture over the meat and put it in the refrigerator. Turn the meat occasionally.

When it is needed for use take it out of the marinade, dry off with a cloth and cut it into smaller pieces, whatever size you want.

The flavor of deer, goat, hare or bear is improved if the meat is larded before cooking with strips of fresh pork fat, about ½ pound to every 4 pounds of meat.

Fried Hare with Sour Cream

[Zayetz Zjarinii v Smetaniye]

1 hare
¼ pound fat bacon, in strips
1 teaspoon salt
3 tablespoons lard or butter for frying
1 cup hot water
1 cup sour cream

Lard the hare with fat bacon strips. Cut it into pieces, salt it and fry in hot fat until it is light brown. Put it into a casserole; swill round the frying pan with the hot water and pour over the meat. Add the sour cream and cook slowly, covered, on top of the stove or in a medium oven, 350°–

400° F., until the meat is tender, approximately between 45–60 minutes. Serve with French-fried potatoes, green beans or beets. *4–5 servings*

Hare Fried in Bread Crumbs

[Zayetz Zjarinii v Suharyach]

1 hare
1 teaspoon salt
1 cup lard or butter
1 carrot
1 onion
1 cup bouillon
Salt and pepper to taste
1 tablespoon flour
1–2 eggs
1 cup bread crumbs

Preheat oven to 400° F. Prepare the hare, salt it and put it in a roasting pan with the fat. Brown it all over. Chop up the carrot and onion and add them, with the bouillon, to the hare. Add salt and pepper. Cover the dish and bake until the meat is tender, approximately 1½ hours. The time will vary with the size of the hare.

When cooked, take it out of the pan—leaving the carrot and onion in the pan—and let it cool. Meanwhile make a gravy by thickening the pan liquid (with carrot and onion) with flour, adding a little more bouillon or water if necessary. Stir well, bring to a boil, then keep warm.

Cut the hare into sections and just before serving dip them into beaten egg, roll in bread crumbs and fry in hot fat for a few minutes. Serve with French-fried potatoes, fresh green salad and tomatoes, with the gravy served separately. *6 servings*

To Roast Wild Goat, Deer, Pig or Bear

[Dikaiya, Koza, Olien, Sviniya, Medveshiye, Myaso Zjarinoe]

Marinade the meat, as in Marinade for Game*, lard it with fat bacon, then roast it in the oven at 450° F. Serve with any vegetables you like.

Fillet of Wild Deer or Goat

[Fille Dikoi Kozi ili Olenya]

Marinade meat as in Marinade for Game*. Lard the meat. Remove the bones from the loin and cut the meat into pieces about 1 inch thick. Pound it lightly, salt it and pan-fry.

PIES AND LITTLE PIES

(PIROGI I PIROSHKI)

Russians apply diminutive names not only to people and animals but also to inanimate objects, even pies. The word *piroshki* (baby pie) is the diminutive of *pirog* or pie.

Pirogi and *piroshki* are widely used in Russia for parties, picnics, lunches, snacks, etc., for a meal on their own or served with soup. There is a great variety of fillings, the most popular being meat, cabbage, fish with *vesiga*,[1] rice with mushrooms, green onions with egg, or mashed potato with bacon. Probably the most famous *pirog* outside Russia is *Kulibiaka*, made with salmon and eaten hot, and found on the menus of most good international restaurants.

Pirogi and *piroshki* are made with short pastry, with

---

[1] *Vesiga* is the dried marrow from the spine of the sturgeon. It is available through The Iron Gate, 424 West 54th Street, New York, N.Y. 10019. Boiled Rice* or Chinese transparent vermicelli, made from green bean starch, may be substituted.

pancake and with yeast dough. They can be served hot or cold. There are also sweet *pirogs* of fruit or berries.

When making any sort of pies or little pies the fillings should be prepared before the pastry is made, not only so that the dough is not kept waiting but to ensure the filling is cold before being put in.

Pie with Fish Filling
[Pirog s Riboi]

For Filling:

1 four-ounce package dry vesiga or transparent Chinese vermicelli
Salted water for boiling vermicelli
1 white onion
4 tablespoons butter
1 pound fresh fish such as cod, snapper, pike, without bones[2]
Pepper to taste
Salt

For Short Pastry:

1 cup softened butter
1 cup sour cream
2 whole eggs
1 egg yolk
1 teaspoon salt
2½ cups plain flour
1½ cups self-rising flour
Butter to grease pie pan
½ cup fine bread crumbs
1 egg for brushing pastry

Preheat oven to 400° F.

Make the filling first. Boil the vermicelli or *vesiga* in *plenty* of salted water—it swells in cooking—for 20 minutes. Drain it well, put it in a bowl and chop with a knife. If real *vesiga* is available (very doubtful) cook according to direc-

---

[2] Canned fish, such as tuna or salmon, could be used instead, with the liquid drained off.

tions on packet or see footnote.[3] Chop the onion finely, fry it in butter and add to the vermicelli. Cut the fish in small pieces and mix in with onion and vermicelli, adding pepper and salt.

Now make the pastry. Put the butter, sour cream, eggs and egg yolk into a bowl, add the salt and mix well together. Fold in first the plain flour, then the self-rising. Mix. Tip the dough out on a well-floured board, knead until smooth and even.

Butter well an oblong pie pan approximately 10 by 12 inches, with sides 1½ to 2 inches high, and sprinkle with half the bread crumbs. Take two-thirds of the dough, roll it out to the size of the pie pan so the dough will line the sides. Flour the dough lightly, roll it over the rolling pin, then unroll into the pie pan, trying not to tear it. Put in the cold filling, spreading it out evenly. Fold in the edges of the dough.

Roll out the rest of the dough and cover the top of the pie, joining all the edges together. Brush with beaten egg and sprinkle with remaining bread crumbs. Make a ½-inch slit in the center to let out steam and prevent the seams opening. Bake for 30–35 minutes until golden brown all over. Take from the oven, cover with grease-proof paper and a cloth and let pie rest for 5 minutes; then slide it onto a board, cut in two lengthwise and across five times. This makes pieces of approximately 2 by 3 inches. Arrange on a dish and serve.
8–10 servings

---

[3] True *vesiga* comes dried or fresh. When fresh it is cooked like vermicelli, in salted water; if dried it must first be soaked for 3–4 hours in cold water.

Little Pies with Spring Onions and Egg Filling
[Piroshki s Lukom i Yaitzami]

For Filling:

1 bunch green onions
2 tablespoons butter
8 hard-cooked eggs
1 teaspoon salt to taste
Pepper

For Short Pastry:

*Dough as for Pie with Fish Filling**

Preheat oven to 350° F.

Make the filling first. Wash the green onions, shake off all the water and cut across into ½-inch pieces. Melt the butter in frying pan and fry green onions for 3 minutes. Chop up hard-cooked eggs very fine. Add green onions with the butter they were fried in, plus salt and pepper, mixing all well together. Let it get cold.

Roll out the dough to less than ¼ inch thickness. Cut it out in circles, using a glass or circular cutter about 3–3½ inches in diameter. Put a full teaspoon of filling in the center of each circle and join the edges together down the middle, forming an oval. Flatten lightly and put on a buttered baking sheet with the seam underneath to prevent opening during cooking. Bake until golden brown, approximately 15–20 minutes. This quantity of dough makes 40–45 *piroshki.*

Yeast Dough Pie with Meat

[Pirog s Myasom]

For Meat Filling:

1 cup water
1 tablespoon salt
½ teaspoon pepper
2½ pounds finely ground beef
½ cup chopped onions
1 tablespoon butter for frying onions
2 tablespoons flour

For Yeast Dough:

1 ounce fresh yeast
½ cup lukewarm water
1½ cups milk
2 eggs
½ cup butter
2 tablespoons oil
1 tablespoon sugar
1 teaspoon salt
5 cups plain flour
1 egg for brushing pastry
1 teaspoon melted butter for brushing pastry

Preheat oven to 350° F.

Make the filling first. Add water, salt and pepper to meat and mix well. Fry onions in butter till light brown. Add meat to onions, mixing all the time to avoid uncooked lumps. Fry about 10 minutes. When meat is almost cooked sprinkle half the flour on it and mix in well; then add the rest of the flour and mix again. Cook for 3 minutes. Remove from stove and leave to cool.

To make the dough, dissolve the yeast in ½ cup warm water. Mix together in a large bowl all ingredients except flour and yeast; then add yeast, then flour. Beat with a wooden spoon for 5–10 minutes, until the dough is thoroughly mixed and starting to form bubbles. It is essential to do this properly or it will be heavy. Cover the bowl with a clean cloth and allow the dough to rise until it has doubled itself in size. Tip it out on a floured board, knead it very lightly, then cut off one-third, reserving this for the top. Roll out the rest of the dough to the shape of a shallow pie pan, about 8 by 10 inches. Allow enough to cover the sides. Lay the dough in the pan, put in the filling, spreading it right to the edges. Turn the edges in over the filling; then roll out the rest of the dough, cover the top of the pie and join the edges together. Make a ½-inch slit in the center, for steam, brush with beaten egg and bake in a moderate oven until the dough is cooked through, about 30 minutes. Test with a cake tester on the edge or corner of the piecrust and if pie is done take it from the oven, brush it with melted butter, cover with grease-proof paper and a light clean cloth. Leave for 5 minutes, then slide it onto a board, cut into oblong pieces and serve hot or cold. *Makes 10–12 pieces*

Deep-fried Little Pies with Cabbage
[Zjarinie Piroshki s Kapustoi]

For Cabbage Filling:

1 medium-sized cabbage
Enough water to cover cabbage
1 white onion
½ cup butter
2 hard-cooked eggs
Salt
Pepper to taste
1 teaspoon sugar

For these *piroshki* the cabbage filling should be made while the dough is rising.

For Yeast Dough:

1 ounce fresh yeast
½ cup lukewarm water
1½ cups milk
1 egg
1 teaspoon salt
1 tablespoon sugar
½ cup oil
3½ cups plain flour
3 cups oil for deep-frying

To make filling, chop cabbage fine, put in saucepan, cover with water and bring to a boil. Cook for 5 minutes. Drain it off in a colander, carefully pressing out any remaining water, otherwise it will be too wet for frying.

Chop the onion and fry in butter till light brown. Add the cabbage and fry together for 10–15 minutes. Chill. Chop the hard-cooked eggs and add to cabbage with salt, pepper and sugar.

To make the dough, dissolve the yeast in ½ cup lukewarm water. Mix together all other ingredients except flour and oil for frying, then add yeast, then flour. Beat with a wooden spoon for 5–10 minutes, until the dough is thoroughly mixed and starting to form bubbles. Do not cut down on the beating time if you want the dough to be light. Cover the bowl with a clean cloth and leave dough to rise. When it has doubled its size, tip out on a well-floured board. Lightly sprinkle flour on top, cut out with a glass into small circles. The dough is very springy and if the glass is pressed straight down on it, it will rise up inside. Cut down into the dough using first one side of the glass, then tilting it to cut with the other, so the air can get out.

Flatten slightly on the board or by patting in your hand into circles 3–3½ inch diameter, then put 1 tablespoon of filling in each. Fold over the dough and join the edges together, forming an egg-shaped pie with the join along the top. Put the *piroshki* on a floured board and let them rise for about 10 minutes.

In a saucepan heat 3 cups of oil to 400° F. for deep-frying. When hot enough drop in a small piece of dough. If it rises to the surface immediately the oil is hot enough. Deep-fry the *piroshki*, 4 or 5 at a time, turning them gently with a fork or pastry tongs, taking care not to pierce them. Cook until golden brown, approximately 5 minutes; take them out, put them on paper toweling to drain and cover with a cloth. Serve hot. *Makes 25–30 piroshki*

Suggested Variations of Fillings:
Mushrooms, Rice and Egg

[Ris s Yaitzami i Gribami]

1 pound fresh mushrooms
1 onion
½ cup butter
*2 cups Boiled Rice**
3 hard-cooked eggs, chopped
1 teaspoon salt
Pepper to taste

Clean, wash and chop the mushrooms. Chop onion and fry in butter. Add the mushrooms and fry until cooked almost dry. Mix with the rice and chopped eggs. Add salt and pepper to taste.

Carrots with Egg

[Morkov s Yaitzami]

1½ pounds carrots, peeled
1 onion
½ cup butter
6 hard-cooked eggs, chopped
1 teaspoon salt
Pepper to taste

Shred the carrots. Chop the onion and fry in half the butter. Add the carrots and the rest of the butter and fry together for 5–7 minutes, stirring lightly. Remove from heat and cool. Add chopped hard-cooked eggs, salt and pepper, mixing well together.

Fried Pancake Pies
[Blinchatiye Piroshki]

For Meat Filling:

½ cup water
1 teaspoon salt
Pepper to taste
1½ pounds finely minced beef
1 large onion
2 tablespoons butter for frying
1½ tablespoons flour

For Pancakes:

3 eggs
1 cup milk
1½ cups plain flour
1 teaspoon salt
¾ cup water
4 tablespoons butter for frying

Make the meat filling first. Add water, salt and pepper to meat and mix well. Chop and fry the onion in butter till light brown. Add meat to onions, mixing all the time to avoid uncooked lumps and fry for about 10 minutes. When almost cooked sprinkle half the flour on meat and mix in well; then add the rest of the flour and mix again. Cook for 3 minutes. Remove from stove and leave to cool.

To make the pancakes, lightly beat the eggs and milk together. Sift the flour and salt together, add to eggs and milk and mix till smooth. Add water and mix again. In a hot frying pan put ½ teaspoon butter. Pour in about 4 tablespoons of pancake mixture and cook on one side, then on the other till light brown. Drain on grease-proof paper. Continue process till all pancakes (*blinchiki*) are made.

Put 1 tablespoon of meat filling on each pancake, not quite in center. Fold over a flap to cover filling, then fold in each side and finally roll up remaining side, making a kind of envelope. Five minutes before serving heat 1 tablespoon of butter in frying pan, put in the pies and brown all over. Serve hot, with broth, or as a light lunch or supper. This quantity makes 12–14 pies. *2–3 pies per serving*

Pancake Pie

[Blinchatii Pirog]

Blinchatii Pirog, a pie with layers of different fillings, is not difficult to make though it has a number of ingredients. Before starting, study the recipe carefully, then prepare the 3 fillings and let them cool while you make the pancakes and finally the pastry covering.

Cook the pie in a cake pan, about 8 inches across and 2½ inches high, with or without removable sides. The *pirog* will come out firm and well shaped and easy to cut.

For Meat Filling:

½ cup water
½ teaspoon salt
Pepper to taste
¾ pound finely ground beef
1 medium-sized onion
2 tablespoons butter for frying
1 tablespoon flour

For Mushroom Filling:

1 tablespoon butter
½ cup chopped onion
2 cups coarsely chopped mushrooms

For Boiled Buckwheat Filling:

*1 cup Boiled Buckwheat**

For Pancake Layers:

2 eggs
¾ cup milk
¾ cup flour
½ teaspoon salt
½ cup water
2 tablespoons butter for frying

For Short Pastry Case:

2 tablespoons softened butter
2 tablespoons sour cream
2 egg yolks
½ teaspoon salt
1½ cups plain flour
1 cup self-rising flour
Butter for greasing pan
¼ cup fine bread crumbs

For Sauce:

1 cup sliced mushrooms, fried in 1 tablespoon butter
1 cup sour cream

Preheat oven to 350° F.

Make the meat filling first. Add water, salt and pepper to meat and mix well. Chop and fry the onion in butter till light brown. Add meat to onion, mixing all the time to avoid uncooked lumps and fry for about 10 minutes. When almost cooked sprinkle half the flour on the meat and mix it in well; then add the rest of the flour and mix again. Cook for 3 minutes. Remove from stove and leave to cool.

Make the mushroom filling. Melt the butter in frying pan, add chopped onion and fry for 2 or 3 minutes, then add chopped mushrooms and fry another 4–5 minutes. Leave to cool.

Prepare the boiled buckwheat.

While the fillings are cooling, make 6 pancakes.

Lightly beat the eggs and milk together. Sift flour and salt together, add to eggs and milk and mix in till smooth. Add water and mix again. In a hot frying pan put ½ teaspoon butter. Pour in about 4 tablespoons of pancake mixture and cook on one side, then turn and cook on the other side till light brown. Drain on grease-proof paper. Continue process till you have made 6 pancakes. Be sure they are not too big to fit into the cake pan.

Make the short pastry case. Put butter, sour cream, egg yolks and salt into bowl and mix well together. Fold in plain flour, then self-rising flour. Mix well. Put dough onto floured board, knead till smooth. Cut off enough dough to cover top of pie and roll out the rest to ⅛ inch thickness, big enough to line the cake pan, including the sides. The dough should be in one piece, without joins. Butter the pan well, sprinkle with fine bread crumbs and line it with the pastry.

Divide the meat filling into 3 parts.

In the cake pan, which is already lined with pastry, spread one-third of the meat filling. Cover with a pancake and put half the boiled buckwheat filling on top. Cover with another pancake, put on half the mushroom filling and cover with next pancake. Repeat, finishing with a top layer of meat.

Roll out the rest of the pastry and cover the top layer. Join the edges securely and bake about 30 minutes in a moderate oven. When cooked, remove the sides from the cake pan and turn pie upside-down on a serving dish. If the pan has no removable sides, just reverse it on to the dish and gently ease the pie out. Serve hot. Cut from the center down, with a sharp pointed knife, like cutting a cake, and pour over the fried mushrooms which have been heated in the sour cream.

This is usually a complete course, but if it is to be eaten with soup the sauce will not be needed. *6–8 servings*

Chicken, Rice and Egg Pie
[Kurnik]

For Filling:

1 boiled chicken weighing about 2 pounds
2 tablespoons butter
*3 cups Boiled Rice**
5 hard-cooked eggs, chopped
1 teaspoon salt
Dash pepper

For Pastry:

*Short Pastry as for Pie with Fish Filling**

For Sauce:

2 cups chicken stock
2 tablespoons flour
½ cup water
2 tablespoons sour cream
Juice ½ lemon

Garniture:

Dill

Preheat oven to 350° F.

Cut up the cooked chicken meat into pieces about 1 inch square and lightly fry them in butter. Mix with the boiled rice and chopped eggs, adding salt and pepper. Chill.

Roll out the pastry, reserving one-third for the pie top. Line an 8 by 10 inch pie pan with pastry and put in the filling. Roll out the rest of the dough, cover the pie and pinch the edges together. Bake for 20–25 minutes. Serve chicken pie hot, cover with sauce and sprinkle with dill.

Sauce:

Boil up the chicken stock. Mix together flour and water and pour into stock, stirring constantly. Add the sour cream. Bring just up to a boil, add lemon juice. *8–10 servings*

Hot Salmon Pie

[Kulibiaka]

Though this famous fish pie is made with the same short pastry as *Kurnik* and other pies it is higher and narrower in shape. It should be made with fresh salmon but canned salmon or tuna can be substituted.

For Filling:

- *1 four-ounce package* vesiga *or Chinese transparent vermicelli*
- *Salted water for boiling vermicelli*
- *1½ pounds salmon fillet*
- *½ cup butter, melted*
- *1 large onion*
- *½ pound mushrooms*
- *1 tablespoon butter for frying*
- *1 tablespoon chopped parsley*
- *3 hard-cooked eggs, chopped*
- *Butter to grease pie pan*
- *1 egg, beaten*
- *¼ cup bread crumbs*

For Pastry:

*Short Pastry as for Pie with Fish Filling**

Optional: 2 tablespoons hot melted butter

Preheat oven to 400° F.

Prepare the *vesiga* or vermicelli. Put it into a large saucepan of salted boiling water (it swells in cooking), reduce heat and boil for 20 minutes. Drain well, put in a bowl and chop up with a knife. Let it cool. If real *vesiga* is used, cook according to instructions on the packet.

Cut the salmon into pieces, coat it in melted butter and allow to cool and stiffen.

Chop the onion and mushrooms. Fry onion in butter;

add mushrooms and toss together. Cool. Add chopped parsley.

Roll out the dough into a large square, about ¼ inch thick. Lay it in a buttered pie pan. Arrange the filling down the center of the dough in layers . . . salmon, *vesiga,* mushrooms with onion and chopped eggs. Fold over the dough, joining it down the center of the pie and forming an oblong. Seal the ends. Make a ½-inch slit to let out steam in cooking. Brush with beaten egg, sprinkle with bread crumbs and bake for 30–35 minutes, till golden brown. If you want to be especially lavish, pour 2 tablespoons of hot melted butter into the slit in the piecrust when you take if from the oven. Cut across into 2-inch pieces and serve hot.

As with most of Russia's best dishes, preparation of *Kulibiaka* is simple but only the finest possible materials are used.
8–10 servings

LIGHT MEALS AND LUNCHEON DISHES

(LYOHKYE BLUDA DLA POSDNEGO ZAVTRAKA)

Though some of the recipes in this chapter may seem similar to those of other countries they taste unmistakably Russian because of such typical ingredients as dill or sour cream or the combination of sour cream and mushrooms. In the same way, though the origins of the stuffed vegetables can be traced back to the Caucasus and Middle East, the fillings have become essentially Russian.

In a Russian household such dishes would be eaten at lunchtime or perhaps some of the stuffed vegetables might be served cold, as *zakuski.* They make a pleasant light meal with a salad and cheese or fresh fruit.

Stuffed Tomatoes

[Farschirovaniye Pomidori]

8 tomatoes
Boiling water

For Veal and Rice Filling:

[Tielyatin s Risom]

½ cup chopped onion
3 tablespoons butter
½ pound ground veal, uncooked
*1 cup Boiled Rice**
½ teaspoon salt
Pepper to taste
¼ cup tomato sauce

Garniture:

½ teaspoon dill or parsley

Choose tomatoes that are ripe but not soft, as even as possible in shape and size. To skin, dip them in boiling water for half a minute, take out with a slotted spoon and peel with a pointed knife. Cut off the top and with a small spoon remove the inside and put it aside. Try not to cut the tomato case.

Stuffed tomatoes should be cooked in the dish in which they are to be served, for they are very soft and may break or lose their shape if handled too much.

To make the veal and rice filling, fry half the onion in 1 tablespoon butter. Add meat and fry together. Take off heat and add boiled rice, salt and pepper. Mix well, add tomato sauce and fill the tomato cases. Put in a casserole. Fry the rest of the onion in remaining butter and add chopped tomato centers. Fry for 5 minutes, then add them round the tomatoes in their dish and simmer for 20 minutes, covered. Sprinkle with dill or parsley and serve hot. *4 servings*

Alternative Fillings:

[All quantities to fill 8 tomatoes.]

Egg and Mushroom

[Yaitza s Gribami]

½ cup chopped onion
3 tablespoons butter
½ pound mushrooms
6 hard-cooked eggs, chopped fine
½ teaspoon salt
Pepper to taste
½ cup bouillon or water
½ cup fresh or sour cream

Garniture:

Dill or parsley

Preheat oven to 350° F.

Fry the onion in 2 tablespoons butter until light brown. Cut up the mushrooms, add to the onion and fry together. Remove from the heat and put aside half the mushrooms. To the remainder add finely chopped hard-cooked eggs, salt and pepper. Mix well and fill the tomato cases. Arrange them upright in an oven-proof dish, add bouillon and the rest of the butter and cook on low heat, covered, for 10 minutes.

Add fresh or sour cream to the rest of the mushrooms, bring them to the boil, pour mixture over the tomatoes and put in the oven for 10 minutes. Sprinkle with chopped dill or parsley and serve. *4 servings*

Fried Fish in Sour Cream Filling

[Riba s Smetaniye]

1 pound fish such as snapper or pike
Salt
½ cup flour
½ cup oil
1½ cups sour cream
½ cup bouillon
2 tablespoons butter

Remove the skin and bones from the fish and cut into pieces. (If using filleted fish it can be fried whole.) Salt it, roll in flour and fry in oil until cooked. Take off the stove and out of the pan, and break up into smaller pieces. Mix in with the sour cream and fill the tomato cases. Arrange them standing upright in a saucepan, add the bouillon and butter and cook gently, covered, for about 15 minutes.

Tomato sauce could be used instead of sour cream. *4 servings*

Peppers Stuffed with Meat

[Pieretz Farshirovanii Myasom]

For Filling:

1 pound finely ground beef	*1 cup water*
*1½ cups Boiled Rice**	*1 teaspoon salt*
½ cup chopped onion fried in 1 tablespoon butter	*Pepper to taste*

8 medium-sized green peppers	*1 cup tomato purée*
2 cups peeled and shredded carrots	*1 cup water*
¼ cup oil	

Make the filling first, by mixing together all the ingredients. Cut the tops off the peppers, remove all seeds, and fill with meat mixture. Stand upright in a saucepan.

Fry shredded carrots in oil for 5 minutes, then add the tomato purée and water. Mix well. Pour over the peppers and bring to a boil. Turn the heat down and simmer for 45 minutes. *4 servings*

Squash Stuffed with Meat
[Kabachok Farshirovanii Myasom]

2 squashes, about 8–10 inches long
Butter for greasing pan
1 teaspoon salt
Dash pepper

For Filling:

1 pound finely ground meat
1 onion fried in 2 tablespoons butter
*1 cup Boiled Rice**
2 cups sour cream

Garniture:

Dill or parsley

Preheat oven to 350° F.

Peel the squashes and cut them into 4 parts, crossways, making slices about 2 inches thick. With a spoon or knife, remove the centers. Set each piece upright, like a cup, on a well-buttered roasting pan. Salt and pepper them lightly.

Mix together the meat, fried onion, boiled rice and add seasoning to taste. Pile into the slices and bake for approximately 30–35 minutes. Pour the sour cream over and leave in the oven for a few more minutes. Sprinkle with dill or parsley. *4 servings*

Squash with Vegetable Filling
[Kabachok Farschirovanii Ovoschami]

*2 squashes, cut and scooped out as for Squash Stuffed with Meat**

For Filling:

½ cup chopped onion
3 tablespoons butter or ½ cup oil
1 cup diced cooked carrots
½ cup diced cooked rutabaga
1 cup diced cooked potatoes
1 teaspoon salt
Pepper to taste
1 tablespoon grated Parmesan cheese
*2 cups White Sauce**

Preheat oven to 350° F.

Fry the onions in butter or oil till golden brown. Add the carrots and rutabaga and fry together for a few minutes. Take off the stove and add the potatoes, salt and pepper. Mix well but do not mash up. Fill the squashes, sprinkle cheese on top and bake in oven about 15–20 minutes, until cooked through and brown on top. Serve with White Sauce*. *4 servings*

Fried Squash

[Kabachok Zjarinii]

1 squash, not too old
½ teaspoon salt
½ cup flour
2 tablespoons butter for frying

Peel the squash and cut into slices about ½ inch thick. Salt them, roll in flour and fry in hot butter till cooked. Serve as accompaniment to meat or as a separate dish. The squash must be young. The same recipe can be used for eggplant, but it should be ripe, otherwise it will have a bitter taste. *2 servings*

Baked Pumpkin with Eggs

[Tikva s Yaitzami]

1 pound fresh pumpkin
½ teaspoon salt
½ cup flour
2 tablespoons butter plus butter to grease baking dish
5 eggs
½ cup milk
Salt and pepper to taste, for eggs
Dill

Preheat oven to 400° F.

Peel the pumpkin and cut it in thin slices. Salt it and lightly roll in flour. Fry in butter until cooked. Arrange in a buttered oven-proof dish which can be brought to the table. Beat the eggs well, add the milk, salt and pepper and pour over the pumpkin slices. Sprinkle with dill and bake in the oven until the eggs are cooked. Serve immediately. *4 servings*

Fried Pumpkin and Spring Potatoes

[Tikva s Kartoschkoi]

1½ pounds pumpkin
½ teaspoon salt
½ cup flour
2 tablespoons butter
1½ pounds small new potatoes
Salted water
½ cup sour cream
Dill

Peel, slice, salt and flour pumpkin as for Baked Pumpkin with Eggs*. Fry it in butter and keep hot. Scrub and boil the potatoes in salted water for about 10 minutes or until cooked. Drain them and put into a serving dish. Arrange the pumpkin on top and pour the sour cream over. Sprinkle with dill and serve as a separate dish or as accompaniment to meat. *4 servings*

Sauerkraut with Mushrooms

[Kvashenaia Kapusta s Gribami]

1 cup dried mushrooms
2 cups water
1 pound sauerkraut
1 cup sour cream
1 teaspoon sugar

Wash the mushrooms, then soak them in 2 cups water for 1 hour. Cook them for 15 minutes in the same water. Take them out and chop them fine. Add them to the sauerkraut with 1 cup of the water in which they cooked. Cook for 20 minutes. Add sour cream and simmer for another 20 minutes. Taste, and if too sour, add 1 teaspoon sugar. Serve hot with meat dishes.

Taste this recipe for salt as you go. *4 servings*

Mushrooms in Cream Sauce

[Gribi v Souse]

½ pound young mushrooms
1 tablespoon butter
¼ teaspoon salt
Dash pepper
*1 cup White Sauce**
½ cup fresh cream
1 teaspoon lemon juice
Dill or parsley

Clean, wash and slice the mushrooms. Put in a pan and fry lightly with butter. Add salt, pepper, white sauce and cream. Simmer, covered, for 5 minutes. Add the lemon juice, sprinkle with dill or parsley and serve as an accompaniment to meat or on toast as a separate dish. 2 *servings*

Fried Mushrooms

[Gribi Zjariniye]

½ pound mushrooms
1½ tablespoons butter
¼ teaspoon salt
Dash pepper

Slice the mushrooms and fry in butter for 6–8 minutes, adding salt and pepper. Serve as accompaniment for meat or as *zakuski* on small pieces of toasted black or white bread. 2 *servings*

Fried Mushrooms with Onion and Sour Cream

[Gribi v Smetaniye]

½ cup chopped onion
2 tablespoons butter
½ pound mushrooms
¼ teaspoon salt
Dash pepper
½ cup sour cream

Fry the onion in butter. Add sliced mushrooms and fry together for 5 minutes. Add salt and pepper and sour cream. Bring to a boil and serve as an accompaniment to meat or as separate dish. 2 *servings*

Egg Nests

[Gniezdo s Yaitzom]

5 eggs
¼ cup milk
4 round slices of brown or white bread, ½ inch thick
2 tablespoons butter for frying
Dill
¼ teaspoon salt
Dash pepper

Preheat oven to 450° F. or broil, depending on how you wish to cook this.

Beat 1 egg with milk. Dip the slices of bread into it and fry on both sides in butter, in preheated pan. Separate yolks and whites of remaining eggs. Beat whites until stiff and arrange like a nest on each piece of bread. Put 1 yolk in the center of each nest, sprinkle with dill, salt and pepper and put under the grill or in a hot oven for a few minutes. 2 *servings*

Scrambled Eggs with Frankfurters

[Yaitchnaya Kashka s Sosiskami]

3 frankfurters
1 tablespoon butter
4 eggs
½ cup milk
¼ teaspoon salt
Dash pepper
Dill
Tomato sauce or 2 fresh tomatoes

Cut frankfurters across into pieces ½ inch thick.

Fry lightly in butter. Beat eggs and milk together and add salt and pepper. Pour over the frankfurters, stirring all the time until cooked. Sprinkle with dill and serve with tomato sauce or fresh slices of tomato.

You could use bacon, ham or salami as variations. *2 servings*

The sauce must be made first so the omelet is not kept waiting.

For Sauce:

1 tablespoon butter
1 tablespoon flour
1 cup hot milk
1½ cups sour cream
2 egg yolks
¼ teaspoon salt
Dash pepper

For Omelet:

4 eggs
½ cup milk
¼ teaspoon salt
Dash pepper
¼ cup chopped dill or parsley
1 tablespoon butter

To make sauce, melt the butter in a saucepan and add the flour, stirring in carefully. Draw off the fire and add the hot milk, stirring to avoid lumps. Mix sour cream and egg yolks together and stir in carefully, adding salt and pepper. Simmer, stirring all the time, until the mixture becomes thick. Do not let it boil.

Beat together all omelet ingredients except the butter. Heat half the butter in frying pan and pour in half the egg mixture. Cook quickly on one side, then turn omelet over and cook other side or put it under broiler to brown. Put on a hot plate and quickly make the second omelet in the remaining butter. Pour the sour cream sauce over each omelet and serve.

2 servings

Eggs in Mashed Potato Rings

[Kartofelnoe Koltzo s Yaitzom]

1 tablespoon butter
1 tablespoon bread crumbs
1½ cups mashed potato
Melted butter for brushing potatoes
4 eggs
¼ teaspoon salt
Dash pepper
4 round slices tomato
Parsley

Preheat oven to 400° F.

Butter a roasting pan and sprinkle it well with bread crumbs. With a pastry tube make four rings of mashed potato, about 3–3½ inches across in the center. Brush them with melted butter, sprinkle with bread crumbs and bake until light brown, approximately 10 minutes. Break one egg into the center of each ring, add salt and pepper and bake until the eggs are cooked, about 7 minutes. Decorate with tomato slices and parsley. Serve hot. *2 servings*

Egg Croquettes

[Kroketi iz Yaitz]

4 hard-cooked eggs
2 raw eggs
½ teaspoon salt
Dash pepper
*¼ cup White Sauce**
1 tablespoon milk
½ cup bread crumbs
2 cups oil or lard for deep-frying
White bread for toast

Mash the hard-cooked eggs thoroughly and mix with one of the raw eggs. Season with salt and pepper and add to the thick white sauce. Roll into small balls the size of a walnut and dip them into the remaining egg, which has been beaten with milk. Roll in bread crumbs and deep-fry for 3 minutes, until golden brown. Serve on small pieces of white toast or piled on a plate as a *zakuska*. *2 servings*

Cottage Cheese Spread with Caraway Seeds
[Tvorog s Tminom]

½ pound unsalted cottage cheese
½ cup butter
1 teaspoon caraway seeds
Salt to taste

Blend the cottage cheese and butter together into a smooth paste. Add caraway seeds, salt and mix well. Serve on toasted black bread or in a glass dish as a *zakuska*. *Makes about ¾ pound*

Buckwheat Kasha
[Grechnevaia Kasha]

Kasha is an important item in Russian cooking. Though the word *kasha* is usually taken to mean boiled buckwheat it is also applied to other cooked grain—to rice (*Risovaia kasha*), semolina (*Mannaia kasha*), oats (*Ovsjanaia kasha*), millet (*Pschonaia kasha*), etc. The closest translation in English is *porridge*. Since boiled buckwheat is so cheap, nourishing and full of vitamins it is widely used. It has been the mainstay of countless poor, old and sick Russians. Its correct name is *Grechnevaia kasha.*

Buckwheat *kasha* is used in substantial dishes or as an accompaniment or stuffing for meat or poultry. It is also used as a breakfast food, prepared as a sweet or savory dish, or boiled and eaten with butter. The Russians say, "Kasha can't be spoiled by too much butter"—"*Maslom kashu nie ispoptisch.*"

Boiled Buckwheat

[Grechnevaia Kasha]

3 cups water
½ teaspoon salt
1 cup buckwheat

Bring the water to a boil, add the salt and pour in the buckwheat, stirring with a spoon. Bring to a boil again, cover, turn down heat and simmer on very low heat for 40 minutes. When ready the *kasha* should be soft right through but not mushy. Each grain should be separate. This quantity makes 4 cups. *4 servings*

There are other ways of making *kasha.* One old *babushka* once surprised her foreign friends by getting up from the table saying, "I go now to get the *kasha* from my bed." Her method was to put the buckwheat into boiling water and boil till the water was evaporated. She then put the lid on tight, rolled the saucepan in thick newspapers, blankets and eider-downs, set it between pillows on her bed and let it finish cooking itself. This is quite common practice and is also used for rice.

Buckwheat with Bacon or Ham

[Kasha s Vetchinoi]

¾ pound bacon or ham
1 tablespoon butter
*4 cups Boiled Buckwheat**
1 hard-cooked egg, chopped

Cut the bacon or ham into 1-inch pieces and fry in butter. Put the boiled buckwheat on a hot dish and lightly mix in the bacon. Sprinkle with chopped egg and serve. As a variation the *kasha* could be eaten with fried onions and butter. *4 servings*

Buckwheat with Cottage Cheese

[Kasha s Tvorogom]

2 cups buckwheat
½ pound cottage cheese
1 teaspoon caraway seeds
1 cup cream

Boil the buckwheat as for Boiled Buckwheat* and as soon as ready mix in the cottage cheese and caraway seeds. Try not to mash it up. Then pour the cream over it and put on very low heat for 10 minutes. Serve hot. *4 servings*

Rice

[Ris]

The Russians use rice a great deal, for garnishing, for soups, for *pilaffs*, for fillings and in sweet dishes. It is used in certain traditional customs, for instance in *Kutija*, served on Christmas Eve at the end of the Christmas Fast, and at Orthodox funerals, when sweetened rice is dealt out to the mourners.

Boiled Rice

[Risovaia Kasha]

1 cup long grain rice
8 cups boiling water
1 tablespoon salt
2 cups boiling water

Drop rice into boiling water, add salt and boil rapidly, uncovered, for 15–20 minutes. Drain water off in colander, then pour 2 cups boiling water over rice to remove the loose starch and separate the grains. Put rice back into saucepan and stand on low heat for 3 minutes to dry out moisture. The grains should be separate.

This makes 4 cups boiled rice. *4 servings*

Pilaff with Mushrooms

[Plov s Gribami]

½ pound mushrooms, sliced
1 onion, chopped
½ cup butter
*3 cups Boiled Rice**
¼ teaspoon salt
Dash pepper

Fry the mushrooms and onion in butter and mix them in with the boiled rice. Add the salt and pepper and stand on low heat in a covered dish for about 10 minutes.

This Russian version of oriental *pilaff*, which came through the Caucasus and wars with Eastern neighbors, could be varied by adding cooked meats, such as roast pork, veal, lamb or poultry, and golden raisins. Russian *plov* differs from Italian *risotto*, Turkish *pilaff* and Spanish *paella* in being made with boiled, not raw, rice. *4 servings*

Pilaff with Egg and Bacon or Ham

[Plov s Yaitzami i Vetchinoi]

2 eggs
¼ cup milk
1½ tablespoons butter
½ pound bacon or ham
*3 cups Boiled Rice**
Salt to taste
Pepper
Dill

Preheat oven to 400° F.

Mix eggs and milk together and make an omelet in the butter. Cut it into small pieces. Cut up the bacon or ham and fry lightly. Mix omelet and bacon with the rice, add salt and pepper, put it in the oven for about 10 minutes in a covered dish. Sprinkle with dill before serving. *4 servings*

Noodles with Cottage Cheese

[Lapscha s Tvorogom]

½ pound broad noodles
5 cups boiling water
1 tablespoon salt
½ pound cottage cheese
2 tablespoons butter

Put noodles in boiling salted water and boil till tender. Drain off and while still hot mix in the cottage cheese and butter. Serve hot. *4 servings*

Noodles, Sailor Style

[Lapscha po Flotski]

½ pound noodles
5 cups boiling water
1 tablespoon salt
½ pound bacon or ham
½ cup chopped onion
2 tablespoons butter
Pepper to taste

Put the noodles into the boiling salted water, boil till tender, then drain off and keep hot. Cut up the bacon or ham, fry the onion in butter and add the bacon or ham. Fry lightly together, then mix in with the noodles. Add pepper to taste and serve hot. *4 servings*

Macaroni Baked with Meat, Egg and Cheese

[Zapekanka s Myasom]

½ pound macaroni
6 cups boiling water
1 tablespoon salt
½ cup chopped onion
1½ tablespoons butter
½ pound ground meat
1 teaspoon salt
Pepper to taste
Butter to grease roasting pan
2 eggs
¼ cup milk
½ cup grated cheese

Preheat oven to 350° F.

Put the macaroni into boiling salted water and boil till tender. Drain off and keep hot. Fry the onion in butter, add the meat and fry together till cooked, stirring to avoid lumps. Add salt and pepper. Mix in with the cooked macaroni and put into a shallow buttered roasting pan or oven-proof dish. Beat the eggs and milk together, pour over the meat, smooth out the top and sprinkle with cheese. Bake until the eggs are cooked, about 20 minutes. Eat hot with ketchup served separately. *4 servings*

SWEET LIGHT MEALS

[Sladkiye Lyohkiye Bluda]

It is not uncommon for a light meal to consist of a sweet dish, nor for these same dishes to be used as a sweet course in a dinner. Most of the following recipes could also be used as desserts.

Sweet Rice

[Risovaia Kasha, Sladnaia]

2 cups milk
½ cup long grain rice
½ teaspoon salt
½ cup sugar
1 tablespoon butter
½ cup golden raisins

Bring the milk to boil. Add rice and salt, boil up again, turn down heat and simmer for 20 minutes, stirring occasionally. Add sugar, butter, raisins. Mix and simmer for 5 minutes. Serve with extra hot milk if desired. *4 servings*

Pilaff with Dried Fruit

[Plov Fruktovii]

½ cup dried apricots
½ cup stoned prunes
½ cup water
½ cup sugar
½ cup raisins
*3 cups Boiled Rice**
1½ tablespoons butter

Wash and cut up the apricots and prunes and cook together with the water, sugar and raisins for 10 minutes in a covered saucepan. Mix the rice with the cooked fruit and their juices, add the butter and serve. *4 servings*

Breakfast Semolina
[Mannaia Kasha]

2½ cups milk
½ teaspoon salt
½ cup semolina
½ cup sugar
1 tablespoon butter

Bring the milk to a boil and add the salt. Pour in the semolina, stirring fast so that no lumps can form. Simmer for 5 minutes, add the sugar and butter and serve hot. The longer you cook semolina the thicker it gets. Remedy this by adding more milk. *2 servings*

Semolina Pudding
[Gurievskaia Kasha]

4 cups milk
½ teaspoon salt
½ cup semolina
1 tablespoon butter
½ cup sugar
½ cup chopped blanched almonds
½ cup golden raisins
½ cup chopped glacéed apricots
Few drops vanilla extract
Few drops almond extract
2 eggs
Sugar for sprinkling on top of pudding

For Apricot Sauce:

1 cup dried apricots
1½ cups cold water
¾ cup sugar

Preheat oven to 500° F.

Bring the milk to a boil in a wide saucepan or casserole, then put it into the hot oven. Watch it carefully and when the top of the milk turns light brown push it down with a wooden spoon so that another top can form. When this is brown, push it down as before. Repeat this 5–6 times, for approximately 20 minutes. Take milk from the oven, bring it to a boil on the top of the stove, add salt and semolina and cook on low heat, stirring all the time, for 10 minutes. Lower oven temperature to 400° F. Add the rest of the ingredients, except the eggs and sugar for sprinkling. Remove from heat. Separate egg yolks and whites. Beat the whites stiff, add the yolks and fold into the semolina mixture. Pour into 6 individual oven-proof dishes, sprinkle with sugar and put into oven for 10 minutes. Serve hot, alone or with apricot sauce.

To make the sauce, wash the apricots in cold water, then put them in 1½ cups of cold water and leave them for 2 hours. Cook them in the same water for 20 minutes. They should be soft. Put them through a fine sieve and then back into their cooking water. Add sugar, bring to a boil, stirring all the time since this burns easily. *6 servings*

Pumpkin Pudding

[Tikvenaia Kasha]

1½ pounds fresh pumpkin
1 cup water
½ cup semolina
2 cups milk
2 eggs
½ teaspoon salt
1 tablespoon sugar
Butter to grease pan
1½ tablespoons melted butter

Preheat oven to 350° F.

Peel and slice the pumpkin. Boil, with 1 cup water, until soft. Drain off excess water, then mash well. Cook the semolina in milk on low heat for 10 minutes. Mix it well with the mashed pumpkin. Separate the egg yolks and whites. Add yolks, salt and sugar to the pumpkin. Beat the whites of the eggs stiffly and fold into the mixture carefully. Put into a well-greased oven-proof dish or small individual dishes. Brush over with melted butter and bake for 20 minutes or until a crust has formed on top. Serve hot. *6 servings*

Macaroni Baked with Fruit

[Zapekanka s Fruktami]

½ pound short macaroni
5 cups boiling water
1½ teaspoons salt
1 tablespoon butter
1 cup diced fresh apples
½ cup golden raisins
½ cup mixed fruit peel
2 eggs
½ cup sugar
1 tablespoon butter for greasing pan
1 tablespoon bread crumbs
½ cup jam

Preheat oven to 350° F.

Put macaroni into boiling salted water, boil till tender; then drain, add 1 tablespoon butter and let it cool. Add apples, raisins and mixed fruit peel. Separate eggs and beat whites stiff. Add sugar and yolks and beat all together. Fold into macaroni and fruit, mixing gently. Put evenly into buttered and bread-crumbed roasting pan and bake for 30 minutes. Serve hot with a teaspoon of jam on each helping. *6 servings*

Yoghurt Pudding

[Varenetz]

4 cups milk
½ cup sour cream
Sugar for sprinkling

Preheat oven to 350° F.

Heat the milk, put it in an oven-proof dish and set it in

the oven. When the top of the milk becomes golden brown and starts to form a crust, push it down with a spoon and stir.

Repeat this process 4 or 5 times so that all the milk is eventually golden brown—about 15–20 minutes. Take it from the oven and let it cool, stirring occasionally. Mix in the sour cream and leave it, at room temperature, until it becomes thick—about 4–5 hours. Put in the refrigerator. Serve cold with sugar sprinkled on top. *6 servings*

Using the same proportions, sour cream could be added to uncooked milk and left to set at room temperature. This makes a kind of yoghurt.

Sweet Vareniki
[Vareniki Sladkiye]

For Berry Filling:

2 cups raspberries, cherries or blackberries
1 tablespoon sugar

For Cottage Cheese Filling:

1 pound fresh unsalted cottage cheese
1 egg
1 tablespoon sugar

For Dough:

3 eggs
2 cups milk
1 teaspoon salt
1½ pounds flour

For Boiling Vareniki:

4 cups boiling water

For Sauce:

1 cup sour cream

To make the berry filling, sprinkle the berries with sugar and leave to stand for 5 minutes. To make cottage cheese filling just mix all the ingredients together.

To make the dough, beat eggs, milk, and salt together in a mixing bowl; add flour, mix well together, with a wooden spoon; turn out on a floured board and knead until springy. Make the *vareniki* in batches, cutting off a section of the dough and rolling it out about ⅛ inch thick. Dust with flour, cut out in 2-inch circles with a glass.

Put 1 teaspoon of filling in the center of each circle, fold in half, pinch edges together. They should be half-moon shapes.

When ready the *vareniki* are dropped into boiling water and cooked till they rise to the surface. Serve 12–15 to each plate, with sour cream poured over. *10 servings*

Sweet Cottage Cheese

[Tvorog so Smetanoi]

½ pound unsalted cottage cheese
½ cup sour cream
1 tablespoon sugar or jam

Optional: 1 cup milk

Put the cottage cheese into a glass dish and pour the sour cream over. Sprinkle with sugar or put some jam on top. You can add milk if you like, half a cup to each serving. This dish is eaten as a light meal in itself and is very popular for breakfast. *2 servings*

Cottage Cheese Patties

[Sirniki]

¾ pound unsalted cottage cheese
2 eggs
½ cup flour
½ cup sugar
1 teaspoon vanilla extract
Flour for dusting
2 tablespoons butter for frying plus butter to grease baking dish
1½ cups sour cream for cooking

Preheat oven to 350° F.

Blend together all the ingredients except the butter for frying and the sour cream for cooking. On a well-floured board, form mixture into round flat cakes about ½ inch thick, 2–2½ inches in diameter. Be sure they are well covered with flour. Melt butter in frying pan and fry *sirniki* on both sides until golden brown. Arrange them flat on a buttered oven-proof dish which can be brought to the table, pour the sour cream over them and bake for 15 minutes.

You could use fresh instead of sour cream and add, with cream, ½ cup golden raisins to give a sweeter flavor.

Sirniki, which look like small thick patties, must be made just before cooking, otherwise they become hard to handle. Once cooked they can be left for reheating just before serving.

4 servings

Sweet Cottage Cheese Paste

[Sladkii Tvorog-pasta]

½ pound unsalted cottage cheese
½ cup sugar
Vanilla extract to taste

If the cheese is lumpy push it through a fine sieve with a wooden spoon, then mix in the sugar and vanilla. Pile it up into a pyramid on a glass plate and serve with stewed, dry or fresh fruit, berries or *Kisel**. *2 servings*

Pancake Pies with Cottage Cheese

[Blinchatiye Piroshki s Tvorogom]

For Pancakes:

3 eggs
1 cup milk
1½ cups plain flour
½ teaspoon salt
¾ cup water
½ cup butter for frying

For Filling:

1 pound unsalted cottage cheese
½ cup sugar
1 egg
Vanilla extract
1 tablespoon butter

For Sauce:

1½ cups sour cream
1 tablespoon sugar

Preheat oven to 450° F.

To make the pancakes, lightly beat eggs and milk together. Sift together the flour and salt, add to egg and milk and mix in till smooth. Add the water and mix again. In a hot frying pan put ½ teaspoon butter, pour in about 4 tablespoons of pancake mixture and cook on one side till light brown. Turn and cook on other side. Drain on grease-proof paper. Continue until batter is used up.

Make the filling by mixing together the cottage cheese, sugar and egg, adding vanilla to taste. Put 1 tablespoon of filling on each pancake, fold over a flap to cover filling, then fold in each side and roll up into a parcel, making a little pie or *piroshki.* Heat 1 tablespoon butter in the fry pan, put in the pancakes and brown all over. When all are fried put them side by side in an oven-proof dish that can be brought to the table, mix together the sour cream and sugar, pour over the *piroshki* and bake for 10 minutes. Serve hot.

These *piroshki* can be served without oven-baking. The sour cream is poured over each one after frying and they are ready to eat. *6 servings*

Apple Charlotte with Egg Sauce

[Scharlotka i Gogol-mogol]

For Charlotte:

Butter for greasing dish
16 bread slices, 4 by 4 by ¼ inch
3 eggs
½ cup milk
1 tablespoon sugar
3 large apples
½ cup raspberry jam
½ cup water

For Sauce:

4 egg yolks
4 tablespoons sugar
1 tablespoon rum
Vanilla extract to taste
2 egg whites

Preheat oven to 350° F.

Butter an oven-proof serving dish about 8 by 8 inches. Toast the bread lightly. Beat the eggs, milk and sugar together. Peel and slice apples, mix jam with the water. Dip four slices of bread into the egg mixture and arrange on the bottom of the dish. Evenly spread one-third of the apples over them and pour one-third of the jam mixture over all. Repeat this twice, covering finally with soaked bread. Bake in oven for 30 minutes. Serve hot or cold.

To make the *Gogol-mogol* sauce, blend the egg yolks with the sugar until the sugar is almost dissolved. Add the rum and vanilla. Beat the egg whites stiff and fold into the yolk mixture. Serve sauce separately. *8 servings*

DESSERTS, COOKIES AND CAKES

(SLADKOYE, PECHENIYE I TORTI)

DESSERTS

[Sladkiye Bluda]

In Russian meals, after *zakuski,* soup and main course, there is usually a pause; then coffee or tea is served, with *torts,* pastries or sweet little cakes.

Russians have an almost oriental love of sweets. Sugared foods and honeyed drinks are mentioned even in the earliest records. This taste may have come from the East or from a natural bodily need for warmth and energy in a cold climate.

Some of the best desserts are made from fruit and berries, and variations of cream cheese mixtures. Most of these are adapted importations from Scandinavia or Germany, as for instance *Kisel,* a fruit-juice pudding which probably came with the Ruriks. It is almost identical with the Danish *Röd Gröd* and is also found in Poland and other Slav countries. *Kisel* may be made from all sorts of berries or fruits, or with flavored milk or water. When using fruit and berries, potato flour is better than corn flour because it does not change color or affect the taste of the juice. It also makes the *kisel* clear.

Kisel is made either thin enough for pouring or thick enough for setting in a mold; but before making either kind the basic fruit juice must be prepared:

Fruit Juice for Kisel

For berries and fruit like black or red currants, cranberries, gooseberries, plums, sour cherries, etc., allow ½ pound sugar to each 1 pound of fruit. For sweeter berries, use less sugar.

Wash the fruit or berries and remove any seeds. Crush with a wooden spoon. Add cold water, just covering the fruit, and simmer for about half an hour, until cooked. Strain thoroughly through a fine sieve, until the liquid is clear. Add the sugar and more water if necessary and bring to a boil; thicken according to requirements.

Kisel *for Pouring*

2 cups sweetened Fruit Juice for Kisel*
1½ tablespoons potato flour or corn flour
½ cup water

Bring the fruit juice for *kisel* to a boil. Mix the potato flour or corn flour with the water and add, stirring all the time. When boiled, take off the stove and use as required.

Rice Pudding with Kisel

[Risovi Puding s Kiselem]

2½ cups milk
½ cup raw rice
Pinch salt
1 tablespoon butter
½ cup sugar
½ cup raisins
¼ cup orange peel
½ teaspoon vanilla
2 eggs—yolks and whites separated
Butter to grease baking dish
Kisel *for Pouring**

Preheat oven to 350° F.

To make the rice pudding, bring the milk to a boil. Add the rice and salt, bring to a boil again, reduce heat and simmer for 10 minutes. Remove from the stove, add the butter, sugar, raisins, orange peel, vanilla and egg yolks. Mix well. Beat the egg whites stiff and fold them in carefully. Put the mixture into an oven-proof buttered dish, smooth over the surface and bake for 15 minutes. Cut into sections or spoon out into individual dessert dishes. Pour the *kisel* over and serve. *6 servings*

Semolina Mold with Kisel

[Mannii Puding s Kiselem]

2½ cups water or 1 cup water and 1½ cups milk
½ teaspoon salt
½ cup semolina
½ cup sugar
1 tablespoon butter
Kisel *for Pouring**

Boil the water, or water and milk. Add the salt. Pour in the semolina, stirring fast to avoid lumps. Simmer for 8–10 minutes, then add sugar and butter. Cook a little longer, until it is really thick, then pour into a 3-cup mold, or small individual molds, rinsed out with cold water. When set, unmold and pour *kisel* over before serving. *6 servings*

Kisel *in Mold with Whipped Cream*

4 cups sweetened Fruit Juice for Kisel*
4 tablespoons potato flour
1 cup water
2 cups fresh cream
1 teaspoon confectioners' powdered sugar

Garniture:
Fresh berries reserved from prepared fruit juice

Bring the fruit juice for *kisel* to a boil, mix the potato flour and water and add to juice, stirring all the time. Boil for 3 minutes. (This makes the *kisel* thicker.) Cool for 30 minutes. Rinse out a 5-cup ring-mold with cold water and pour in the mixture. Let it set.

Whip the cream with the sugar. Unmold the *kisel*, fill the center with cream and decorate with fresh berries. *6 servings*

Coffee Parfait

[Parfe Koffeinoe]

2½ cups fresh cream
½ cup freshly ground coffee
6 egg yolks
1 cup sugar
1 tablespoon gelatin
½ cup warm water

Bring the cream to a boil. Add coffee, cover and put aside for 30–45 minutes. Blend egg yolks and sugar together. Add strained coffee-cream. Dissolve the gelatin in warm water and pour it into the coffee mixture. Mix it in well. Rinse out a 5-cup mold with cold water, put in the coffee-cream and stand in the refrigerator or freezer until it is set. It could be frozen like ice cream or eaten just set firm. Unmold before serving. *8 servings*

Fruit Surprise

[Fruktovii Surpris]

1 can fruit cocktail, 1-pound-14-ounce size, and juice from can
3 eggs
¾ cup sugar
1 tablespoon gelatin
¼ cup warm water
2½ cups sour cream
½ teaspoon almond extract

Open can and separate fruit from juice. Separate the eggs and blend the yolks with the sugar. Dissolve the gelatin in the warm water. Put 1½ cups of the fruit juice, egg yolks and sugar and gelatin into a saucepan and heat, stirring all the time. Do not boil. Remove from the heat and chill. Beat the whites of the eggs stiff, add the sour cream and almond extract. Beat again; then add to the chilled mixture. Mix together well. Add the fruit. Mix lightly. Rinse out an 8-cup mold with cold water, put in the mixture and allow to set. *8 servings*

Ice Cream

[Plombir]

3 cups fresh cream
1½ tablespoons confectioners' powdered sugar
1 teaspoon vanilla extract
½ teaspoon almond extract
½ cup chopped glacéed cherries
1 cup chopped glacéed pineapple
½ cup chopped blanched almonds

Whip the cream and add the sugar, vanilla and almond extract. Fold in the glacéed fruit and almonds, put the mixture into a 5-cup mold or into individual dessert dishes and freeze until hard. Unmold by dipping the mold into warm water for a few seconds. Cut into sections with a warm knife and serve. *8 servings*

COOKIES AND CAKES
[Pecheniye i Torti]

Branches
[Hvorost]

Hvorost are like Swedish Klenäter (Christmas crullers) but are eaten without jam. They probably came from Scandinavia. The Russians always serve them at Christmas. They look rather like branches covered with snow and taste delicious.

4 egg yolks
⅓ cup fresh cream or canned milk
¼ cup brandy
1½ teaspoons confectioners' powdered sugar
1½ cups plain flour
3 cups oil for deep-frying
Confectioners' powdered sugar for dusting

Mix together all ingredients except frying oil and dusting sugar. Stir until well blended. Turn the dough onto a floured board, knead, roll out very thin, rather less than ⅛ inch thick. With a pastry wheel cut strips about ¾ inch wide and 3 inches long. Cut a slit in the center of each strip and twist one end through, making a kind of loose loop. Fry in deep oil, a few at a time, at about 375° F., until light brown.

Put on a serving dish and dust with powdered sugar while

still hot. Pile them into a heap, dusting them as they come from the pan. Do not handle too much, they break easily. *Makes approximately 3 dozen*

Little Stars

[Zvesdochki]

4 egg yolks
1 cup sugar
1 teaspoon vanilla
1 cup unsalted butter
4 cups self-rising flour
Butter to grease baking sheet

Preheat oven to 350° F.

Blend together the egg yolks and sugar. Add the vanilla. Melt the butter and add slowly. (It should not be *hot.*) Fold in the flour. The mixture should be quite firm. Put it into the refrigerator for an hour. Roll out to ¼ inch thickness and cut the *zvesdochki* with a star-shaped cutter. Arrange on greased baking sheet. Bake until golden brown, approximately 10 minutes. *Makes 3 dozen cookies*

Almond Fingers

[Mindalniye Palchiki]

1¼ cups plain flour
3 tablespoons blanched and grated almonds
½ cup confectioners' powdered sugar
4 tablespoons unsalted butter
Vanilla to taste
Butter for greasing pan
Flour for dusting
1 cup confectioners' powdered sugar for dusting cookies

Preheat oven to 250° F.

Mix together all ingredients except butter for greasing and dusting flour and sugar. Mix with a knife on a pastry board, then knead as lightly as possible. Carefully, with the help of a knife, shape into little crescents about 1½–2 inches long. Do not use a cookie cutter; the crescents should not be flattened. Put them on a buttered baking sheet, dust with flour and bake for about 30 minutes. Watch them carefully to see they do not burn. Take them out and while still hot, dust and roll in confectioners' powdered sugar. Let them cool on a wire tray. *Makes approximately 2½ dozen cookies*

Trumpets with Cream

[Trubotchki so Slivkami]

4 egg whites
2 egg yolks
1 tablespoon unsalted butter, softened
½ cup sugar
¾ cup flour
Butter for frying
2½ cups fresh cream for filling
Confectioners' powdered sugar for dusting

Beat the egg whites stiffly. Cream the yolks, butter and sugar together. Add flour. Mix well, then fold in the egg whites. Heat frying pan, brush with melted butter and pour in about 2–3 tablespoons of the mixture, like a thin pancake. Fry lightly. Turn over and cook on the other side for a few minutes. Remove to a board, cut pancake in halves and while still hot form each half into a trumpet or cone. Chill. Repeat process until all the mixture is used. Just before serving whip about 2½ cups of fresh cream and fill the trumpets. Dust with confectioners' powdered sugar. *Makes 12–14 trumpets*

Cream Puffs

[Pirojnoe Zavarnoe s Zavarnim Kremom]

1 cup oil
2 cups boiling water
2 heaped cups plain flour
1 teaspoon sugar
Pinch salt
6 eggs (if small use 8 eggs)
Butter for greasing pan

Boiled Cream Filling:

5 cups milk
4 eggs
2 cups sugar
1 cup flour
1 teaspoon vanilla
½ cup unsalted butter
1 tablespoon confectioners' powdered sugar for dusting

Preheat oven to 400° F.

To make the cream puffs, boil the oil and water together. Remove from the heat and add flour, stirring in rapidly. Add sugar and salt. While still hot beat in eggs, one at a time, mixing well after each addition. Allow to cool for 2–3 hours, if possible in the refrigerator. On a greased baking sheet drop spoonfuls of mixture, about the size of half an egg or a large walnut. (Use a pastry tube if possible.) Bake for 30–40 minutes. Do not open oven door for the first 20 minutes, while the puffs are rising, or they may collapse.

When cooked, cool them on a wire tray, then cut open at one side and add filling.

To make filling, boil 4 cups of the milk. Blend the eggs and sugar together and add the rest of the milk, flour and the vanilla. Add this to the hot milk and pour into the top of a double boiler over boiling water. Bring to a boil and keep boiling, stirring until thick. Cool till lukewarm. Beat in an electric mixer or by hand until creamy, adding butter. Be sure it is thoroughly blended. The butter should be warmed before adding to facilitate melting in.

When the filling is cold, put it into the cold cream puffs and dust with powdered sugar. *Makes 30–35 puffs*

Napoleon

[Napoleon Tort]

3½ cups plain flour
2 cups butter, at room temperature
1 cup sour cream
Butter to grease baking sheet
*Boiled Cream Filling**
Confectioners' powdered sugar for dusting

Put the flour on a board and cut the butter into it with a knife. Continue to cut till there are no large pieces of butter left. Add the sour cream and cut again, until all the flour is absorbed. Roll up the dough into a ball and put in the refrigerator overnight or for 12 hours. Then divide into 4 parts.

Preheat oven to 425° F.

On a floured board, roll each part of dough separately, to about the same shape, making 4 layers, about ⅛ inch thick. Bake each layer separately on a flat buttered baking sheet about 14 by 10 inches, for 10–12 minutes. The layers should be light golden in color. Cool them and prepare the Boiled Cream Filling*. Spread it evenly on each layer, putting one on top of the other, finishing with cream. Trim the edges with a sharp knife. Crumble up the cut off edges and sprinkle on top of cream. Dust with confectioners' powdered sugar.

If you prefer, whipped fresh cream with a little sugar could be used instead of boiled cream. *Makes about 24 pieces*

Fruit Cake

[Mazurka]

This is another Christmas specialty, though it is also eaten at any time during the year. It is like Christmas cake only it is made without spirits and with less flour. It is a flat shallow cake which does not rise at all. The eggs, flour and honey are mainly used to bind the fruit together. A good *mazurka* is rather moist.

2 cups mixed dried fruit—raisins, golden raisins, currants, etc.
1 cup dates }
1 cup dried figs }
½ cup glacéed cherries } *cut into ½-inch pieces before measuring*
½ cup glacéed pineapple }
1 cup mixed glacéed peel }
1 cup blanched almonds, cut into threes before measuring
3 eggs
½ cup honey
1½ cups flour
Butter to grease paper for baking

Preheat oven to 250° F.

Mix together thoroughly all ingredients except butter for greasing. Spread well-buttered grease-proof paper on a shallow baking pan, about 10 by 14 inches; then put in the mixture, patting it out about ¾ inch deep. Cook in a slow oven for about 1 hour, until golden brown. Cool. Remove the paper. Cut into strips about 2 by ½ inches.

Mazurka, which is excellent with coffee, will keep for 2–3 weeks in the refrigerator if put in an airtight container. *Makes about 60 pieces*

Mikada

[Mikada]

2 tablespoons butter, softened
2 eggs
1 cup sugar
1 cup sour cream
5 cups plain flour
1 teaspoon baking powder
1 cup extra flour for the board
*Boiled Cream Filling**

Preheat oven to 400° F.

Cream the butter, eggs and sugar together, then add the sour cream. Sieve together the flour and baking powder and add to mixture, mixing all together. Take a little of the dough and on a very well-floured board roll it out to ⅛ inch thickness, either oblong or round. The dough is very sticky and brittle so use plenty of flour. Bake this first layer on a flat baking sheet lined with grease-proof paper until it is light brown, about 10 minutes. Take it from the oven, slide it off the sheet without removing the paper, and chill.

Repeat this process for the next layer, rolling, baking and chilling, and continue until all the dough is used—about 8 or more small layers.

Make a Boiled Cream Filling*. Let it get cold, then spread it on the first layer of cake, about the same thickness as the cake layer. Repeat this process till all the cake layers and cream are used, finishing with a layer of cream on top.

The cake layers are very brittle, so if they start to break up in handling join them together as best you can. The cream filling will stick them together. *Makes approximately 18 pieces*

Sponge Cake with Butter Cream

[Tort Biskvitnii s Maslyanim Kremom]

This basic sponge cake can be used for different *torts.* Either make it in two cake pans, about 8 inches in diameter, or in one deep one, cutting it in four layers when cold to add filling.

Butter for greasing pans
4 large or 6 small eggs
1 cup fine granulated sugar
1 cup flour
2 teaspoons baking powder
1½ tablespoons butter
4 tablespoons water

For Butter Cream:

2 cups unsalted butter
1 cup fine granulated sugar
1 cup canned unsweetened evaporated milk
1 teaspoon instant coffee dissolved in 1 tablespoon hot water

For Moistening Cake:

1 teaspoon instant coffee dissolved in ½ cup warm water
1 tablespoon coffee liqueur
1 tablespoon sugar

Preheat oven to 350° F.

To make the sponge cake, prepare the cake pans by greasing with butter. Separate the yolks and whites of the eggs. Beat the yolks until well mixed; beat the whites till stiff. Add sugar gradually to the egg whites, beating till the mixture is thick. Add egg yolks and beat till absolutely stiff. Add flour and baking powder sifted together, folding in lightly with an egg whisk. Heat the butter and water together to boiling point and fold in carefully to mixture. Pour into greased pans and bake for 20 minutes.

If there is no time to bake the sponge cake yourself a bought one will suffice.

To make the butter cream, blend together butter and sugar. Blend in milk gradually, 2 tablespoons at a time, mixing between each addition. When the milk is all in and the butter cream is almost white, add the coffee mixture.

Mix together ingredients for moistening cake.

Cut the cake into 4 layers. Moisten the first layer with the coffee-liqueur liquid, then spread the cream over it. Put second layer on top and repeat moistening and spreading. Repeat with each layer. Use two-thirds of the cream for the layers, reserving the rest to cover top and sides and for decoration, using a frosting tube. *Makes 12 generous slices*

Sponge Cake with Fresh Cream and Pineapple

[Tort Biskvitnii so Slivkrami i Ananasom]

*1 sponge cake, bought or made as for Sponge Cake with Butter Cream**
2 cups fresh cream
1 tablespoon confectioners' powdered sugar
1 one-pound can pineapple pieces. Reserve liquid
Few red glacéed cherries

Cut the cake into 4 layers. Whip the cream with the sugar. Moisten the first sponge layer with 2 tablespoons of liquid from the pineapple, then spread one-quarter of the cream and put pieces of pineapple on it. Put second layer on top, moisten and spread in same way. Continue till all layers are used, ending with cream and cherries and pineapple pieces arranged in a pattern on the top.

This cake could be made with canned peaches, strawberries, raspberries or with fresh fruit. The canned fruit has a stronger flavor. *Makes 12 generous slices*

Walnut Cake

[Orechovii Tort]

5 eggs
1 cup walnuts
½ cup butter
1 cup sugar
½ cup milk
2 cups self-rising flour
Butter to grease cake pan
1 tablespoon bread crumbs

For Walnut Butter Cream:

2 cups unsalted butter
1 cup fine granulated sugar
1 cup unsweetened canned milk
½ cup fine walnut crumbs
½ teaspoon walnut extract
12 walnut halves

Preheat oven to 350° F.

Separate egg yolks and whites. Grind the walnuts. Cream the butter, sugar and egg yolks together. Add milk and walnuts, mix well and blend in the flour. Beat whites of eggs till stiff, then fold into the mixture carefully.

Butter and bread crumb a 10-inch round or square cake pan, put the mixture into it and bake for 30 minutes. Test by inserting a cake tester and if it comes out sticky leave the cake in the oven for a few more minutes. When cooked, let it stay in the pan for 5 minutes, then put it on a board and let it cool. The cake should be absolutely cold before putting on the butter cream.

To prepare the walnut butter cream, blend together butter and sugar. Add milk gradually, blending in 2 tablespoons at a time, mixing between each addition. Before adding the flavoring, set aside enough of the white cream for decorating—

approximately 1 cup; then add the walnut crumbs and walnut extract to the rest of the mixture. Cut the cold cake into 4 layers and spread the cream on each layer, leaving enough to cover top and sides. Arrange layers one on top of the other. Decorate with the white cream forced through a frosting tube and with the walnut halves. Serve with coffee or tea. *Makes 12 generous slices*

Pavlova Meringue Cream Cake

[Tort à la Madame Pavlova]

1 cup egg whites	*Butter to grease baking sheet*
2 cups fine granulated sugar	*2 cups cream*

Preheat oven to 200° F.

Beat the egg whites very stiff, then add the sugar gradually, about 2 tablespoons at a time. Continue beating till all the sugar is used. Drop the mixture from a tablespoon onto a buttered baking sheet. Cook in a very slow oven for at least 2 hours, until the meringues are dried out. Let them cool. This makes about 30 meringues. They can be made any time and kept in an airtight container until needed. (Allow 2 meringues for each person.)

Whip the cream. Spread a thin layer on a plate or serving dish and on it arrange a layer of meringues. Since it is hard to arrange meringues in layers, put a tablespoon of cream on each meringue and build up the others into a dome-shaped cake. Leave for 1 hour, then serve.

This *tort,* which is as beautiful and light as Pavlova dancing, has an extravagant Byzantine appearance which adds interest to a party table. *Makes 12–15 servings*

Cottage Cheese Tart
[Vatrushki]

This recipe can be made as small tarts or as one big tart cooked in a pie pan.

For Dough:

3 egg yolks
½ cup sugar
4 tablespoons unsalted butter
1 cup sour cream
1½ cups self-rising flour
½ cup plain flour
Butter to grease pie pan

For Filling:

1 pound unsalted cottage cheese
1 tablespoon unsalted butter
½ cup sugar
2 tablespoons sour cream
3 egg yolks
½ cup golden raisins
1 egg, beaten, for brushing

If Making One Big Tart:

1 egg white for brushing
1½ cups fresh cream
1 tablespoon confectioners' powdered sugar

Preheat oven to 350° F.

To make the dough, blend the egg yolks, sugar and butter. Add the sour cream, mix and add all the flour. Knead lightly on a floured board. Roll out the dough to ¼ inch thickness and cut it into circles about 4 inches in diameter. (See below for one big tart.)

Make the filling by putting the cottage cheese through a fine sieve, then mix it in with the butter, sugar, sour cream, egg yolks and raisins. Soften the butter first so it mixes in easily. Put the filling into the center of the pastry circles. Lift the edges and pinch them with your fingers in 6 or 8 places. Brush with beaten egg and bake for about 15–20 minutes. Serve cold.

If making one big tart, put the dough in a buttered pie pan about 10 by 12 inches, brush with white of egg and bake for 5 minutes. Take out and quickly spread the cottage cheese mixture evenly in the tart, put back into oven at once and bake for 20–25 minutes. When cold, whip cream with sugar and spread on top, cut into sections and serve. *Makes approximately 18 small tarts or servings*

Open Apple Pie

[Yablochnii Pirog]

*Dough made as for Cottage Cheese Tart**
1 egg white for brushing
Butter to grease pie pan

For Filling:

3 egg whites
1 cup fine granulated sugar
1 can pie apples, 1 pound 14 ounces size

Alternative accompaniments: ice cream or whipped cream

Preheat oven to 300° F.

Roll out the dough and put it into a buttered pie pan, approximately 10 by 8 inches. Brush with egg white, put into oven for 5 minutes. Meanwhile, to make filling, whip remaining egg whites stiff. Add sugar. Take pastry from the oven, spread in the apple, cover with whipped egg white and bake for 20 minutes. Serve hot with ice cream or cold with whipped cream. *Makes approximately 18 servings*

Rum Baba

[Romavaya Baba]

Baba has been described as the only true Russian cake; plain *baba,* baked in a high tin without a central hole, is a traditional Easter cake, yet it is also known to have come from Poland, where it was originally made of rye flour and moistened with sweet Hungarian wine. *Baba* is also made in Turkey and *Baba au Rhum* is an international menu item. This variation is said to have been invented by King Stanislaus of Poland, who first dipped his *kugelhopf* into rum. *Kugelhopf* was made from very early times at Lvov.

2 ounces fresh (compressed) yeast
1 cup lukewarm water
1 cup sugar
1 cup butter
3 eggs
½ teaspoon salt
Vanilla, rum, lemon extracts to taste
4 cups flour
1 cup golden raisins

For Rum Syrup:

1 cup sugar
1 cup water
¼ cup rum

Preheat oven to 350° F.

Dissolve the yeast in 1 cup of lukewarm water. Blend sugar, butter and eggs together. Add salt and flavoring extracts. Add yeast. Mix well, add flour and beat with a wooden spoon till bubbles start to appear. Add the raisins. The longer the beating the better and lighter the *baba* will be.

Cover the mixing bowl with a clean cloth and leave the dough to rise until it has doubled in size. Beat lightly and put into a buttered *baba* pan about 10 inches high, 6 inches wide, with a 2-inch hollow center. If you cannot get this traditional *baba* mold, use a 2-pound fruit, coffee or shortening can with the top cut off neatly.

Baba can also be made in a Turk's Head mold, called in France *moule en couronne*. For such a mold measuring 8 by 5 inches, use half the ingredients given here.

Leave the *baba* to rise in the pan or can for 30 minutes, then bake for 25–40 minutes. Test with a long wooden cake tester and if it comes out dry the *baba* is ready.

Take it from the oven and leave it to cool in the pan or can for 30–45 minutes; then turn it out carefully. Let it cool completely, for at least 4 hours, before pouring the rum syrup all over, soaking it thoroughly. Traditionally, it is cut into sections from top to bottom, for serving, but these long strips could be cut in halves crossways.

To make the syrup, bring the sugar and water to a boil, add the rum and allow to cool before using.

For a stronger flavor, use rum extract; for variation use *Kirsch*. *14–16 servings*

Krendel

[Krendel]

This is a sweet, enriched bread which is traditionally made for Name Days, also brought to friends' houses when visiting. In appearance it is rather like the Scandinavian butter cakes and Continental sweet breads.

1 ounce fresh (compressed) yeast
½ cup warm water
2 eggs
1 cup sugar
1 tablespoon butter
½ cup milk
3½ cups flour
½ cup golden raisins
½ pound very cold butter
Butter to grease baking pan
1 small egg
¼ cup sugar

Preheat oven to 350° F.

Melt the yeast in the warm water. Blend eggs, sugar and butter together. Add milk, then yeast, and mix. Add flour and beat well. Add raisins, mixing them in lightly. Cover the mixing bowl with a cloth and let the dough rise to double its bulk; then put it on a very well-floured board and flatten it with your hand to ¼ inch thickness. Slice the cold butter to ⅛ inch thickness, cover half the dough and bring the other half over, covering the butter, then fold in three. Roll out to ½ inch thickness and fold in three again. Roll again. Repeat twice. Then roll the dough into a long roll and twist it several times, like a rope. Form it into a big B shape and put it into a buttered baking pan, about 8 by 10 inches, 2 inches deep, or on a flat baking sheet. Let it rise again to double its size, then brush with beaten egg and sprinkle top with sugar. Bake for 30–35 minutes. Test with a cake tester and if it comes out dry the *krendel* is cooked.

Take it out of the oven and leave it on baking sheet for 10 minutes, then put it on a rack and let it cool before cutting into sections. *Makes 20–25 pieces*

MARINADED FRUIT AND VEGETABLES. SAUCES.

(MARINOVANIYE FRUKTI I OVOSCHI. SOUSA)

Marinaded Fruit

[Marinovaniye Frukti]

Originally used to preserve fruit and vegetables out of season and supply a source of winter vitamin foods, marinades are also eaten for their fresh and pleasant taste, as an accompaniment to meat and to freshen the palate during a large meal. They go very well with *shaslik* or poultry.

In Russia, oak leaves are sometimes put into dill pickles to make them firm and black currant leaves are added to give a pleasant scent.

The following marinade is used for apples, pears, quinces, grapes and cherries. If the jars are kept in a cool place or in the refrigerator the fruit will last for months.

6 cups water
2 teaspoons cloves
½ teaspoon peppercorns
5–6 bay leaves
3 cups sugar
½ stick cinnamon
1½ ounces acetic acid, 33.33 strength

Boil all the ingredients together for 5 minutes. Chill. Take out the cinnamon stick before pouring marinade over the fruit.

This amount of marinade is enough for a ½-gallon jar of fruit.

To prepare apples and pears for marinade. Wash the fruit. Put it in cold water. Bring to a boil and cook for 3 minutes. Watch the fruit so that the skin does not crack. Take out of boiling water, leaving fruit whole or cut in halves. Pour the marinade over and leave for 2 days.

To prepare quinces. Peel and cut into long pieces. Boil until soft. Strain well. Pour marinade over.

To prepare cherries and grapes. Make the marinade. Bring it to a boil. Drop in the washed fruit and remove from heat. Chill, then pour into jars. May be eaten in a day or two.

Marinaded Vegetables

[Marinovaniye Ovoschi]

Marinaded Beets

[Marinovanaya Svekla]

Make the marinade as for Marinaded Fruit*, using 1 cup instead of 3 cups of sugar.

Cook the beets whole, in skins, until soft, then remove skins. (Be careful not to overcook.) Put them in a jar and pour the marinade over.

The same recipe is used for pumpkin.

Button Mushrooms or Mushroom Stalks

[Marinovaniye Gribi]

10 cups water
Juice 1 lemon
2 pounds mushrooms or mushroom stalks

Make marinade as for Marinaded Fruit using 1 cup instead of 3 cups sugar*

If using mushroom stalks, cut them in ½-inch sections. Button mushrooms are left whole.

Heat the water and when boiling add the lemon juice and the mushrooms or stalks. Boil for 2–3 minutes, then take out the mushrooms with a perforated spoon and put them immediately into cold water. This makes them crisp. Let them cool, then put mushrooms into a colander, pressing slightly to extract excess water. Put into a jar and pour marinade over.

Marinaded Cabbage

[Marinovanaya Kapusta]

For Marinade:

1 cup vinegar
3 cups water
1 cup sugar
3 bay leaves
Few peppercorns and cloves

2 pounds cabbage
1 tablespoon salt

Boil the marinade ingredients together and chill.

Shred the cabbage very thin, sprinkle it with salt and mix well on a board, lightly rubbing in the salt. Put into a glass jar, pour the marinade over and leave in the refrigerator for 2–3 days. Serve with cold meat, *shaslik* or as a *zakuska.*

Light-salted Cucumber

[Malosolniye Ogurtzi]

These are salted, not preserved, and will only keep for a week to 10 days. For longer preservation a different method, given below, is used.

10 young cucumbers, about 5–6 inches long	*Bay leaf*
1 large spray dill	*Peppercorns*
3–4 cloves garlic	*12 cups water*
	3 tablespoons salt

Slice both ends off young cucumbers and slit the skins lengthwise in about 6 to 8 places.

Put them into a heat-proof container. Add the dill—stalk and leaves—garlic, bay leaf and peppercorns. Boil the water with the salt and pour over the cucumbers. They should be well covered. They will float but push them down, packing them in securely, if necessary putting a weight on top. They will be ready to eat next day. Keep in the refrigerator.

Salted Cucumber

[Soleniye Ogurtzi]

For Salting Liquid:

12 cups water
6 tablespoons salt
2½ cups vinegar
10 young cucumbers, about 5 inches long, approximately the same shape
1 large spray dill
Few peppercorns
3–4 cloves garlic
Few mustard seeds
1 horseradish root
10–15 oak leaves (if obtainable)

Boil together the water, salt and vinegar. Let it cool thoroughly.

Wash the cucumbers. On the bottom of a 12-cup earthenware jar put a layer of dill, peppercorns, garlic, mustard seed, horseradish and an oak leaf. On top tightly pack a row of cucumbers. Put in another layer of seasonings, then more cucumbers, making as many layers as you need and ending with the seasonings. Put a weighted board on top and pour the cold salted water over the cucumbers. Keep in a cool storage room for 25–30 days, until matured. They will last for several months if kept cool.

Green or half-ripe tomatoes could be salted in the same way.

Dill Pickled Cucumbers

[Marinovaniye Ogurtzi]

These are very popular in Russia, not only because cucumbers grow so freely but because they provide vitamins during winter months when fresh vegetables are scarce.

Choose small cucumbers, no more than 2–2½ inches long.

For Marinade:

5 cups water
1 ounce acetic acid, 33.33 strength
½ teaspoon cloves
1 teaspoon peppercorns
4–5 bay leaves
1½ teaspoons salt
1½ teaspoons sugar

3 dozen small cucumbers
Saucepan boiling water
Large spray dill

Boil the marinade ingredients together and chill.

Wash the cucumbers, put them in a sieve or colander and submerge them in a saucepan of fast-boiling water for 3–5 seconds. Lift out and immediately put into cold water. This makes them crisp and preserves their natural color.

Put the cucumbers into a glass jar in layers with dill between each layer. Pour the marinade over. Leave for 5–6 days. This will keep for 4 or 5 months in a cool storage room, or it can be eaten at once.

Sauces

[Sousa]

Many of the sauces used in Russian cooking are direct imports from France and are found in any general cookbook. Those given here are more typically Russian.

Horseradish
[Hren]

½ pound horseradish
1 tablespoon white wine vinegar
Salt to taste

Thoroughly clean horseradish roots, then grate on a fine grater. Mix in with vinegar and add salt to taste. *Makes 1½ cups*

Horseradish with Beets
[Hren so Svekloi]

*½ cup ready-made Horseradish**
¼ cup Marinaded Beets, finely chopped*

Mix together thoroughly. *Makes ¾ cup*

Horseradish and Sour Cream Sauce
[Hren so Smetanoi]

*1 cup ready-made Horseradish**
½ cup sour cream

Mix together thoroughly. This is much milder than ordinary horseradish. *Makes 1½ cups*

Mustard
[Gorchitza]

½ cup mustard powder
½ cup sugar
1 teaspoon salt
Little boiling water
Juice ½ lemon

Mix together the mustard, sugar and salt, adding enough boiling water to moisten. Add the lemon juice and mix again. *Makes 1 cup*

Gravy for Meat or Poultry
[Sousa Myasnoi]

After roasting meat or poultry, strain off excess fat from the pan, heat the remaining juices and add 2 tablespoons of sour cream. Stir in well, boil and serve in a sauceboat.

Mayonnaise
[Provençal]

2 egg yolks
1½ cups oil
1 teaspoon salt
1½ teaspoons sugar
Juice ½ lemon

Put the raw yolks in a mixing bowl. Stir, adding oil, a few drops at a time, until almost all is used. Add salt, sugar, lemon juice and continue to stir, adding the rest of the oil. *Makes 2 cups*

White Sauce

[Bieli Sous]

3 tablespoons butter	*½ cup sour (or fresh) cream*
2 tablespoons flour	*Salt and pepper*
2 cups milk	*Chopped dill*

Melt the butter, add the flour and stir until blended. Add the milk slowly, stirring all the time to avoid lumps. Draw the saucepan off the fire when adding milk. Cook slowly for about 10 minutes. Add the sour cream (or fresh cream if preferred), salt and pepper. When serving, sprinkle with chopped dill. *Makes 3 cups*

Sour Cream and Mushroom Sauce

[Smetanii Sous s Gribami]

1 cup chopped onion	*½ teaspoon salt*
2 tablespoons butter	*Dash pepper*
½ pound mushrooms, sliced	*1½ cups sour cream*

Fry onion in butter. Add the sliced mushrooms. Season. Fry together for 5–10 minutes. Add sour cream and bring to a boil. *Makes 3 cups*

SPECIAL OCCASIONS

The Russian love of gaiety turns traditional feasts and celebrations into lively affairs. The beginning of Lent, Easter, Christmas, family birthdays and Name Days are always good for a party, and weddings, christenings, anniversaries and picnics help to fill up the year.

Russian parties are always good. The table is loaded with poultry and hams, fish and aspics, brawns and salads of all kinds, with compotes of marinaded fruits spaced out between. Everyone helps himself or each other, which means that the hostess can preside at the table instead of spending a hot resentful evening in the kitchen.

If there are a great many guests the supper or dinner may be *à la fourchette*, but most people are happier round a long table, because it is better for toasting, a vital part of Russian gatherings.

Toasting is constant and enthusiastic—the guest of honor, the patron saint, Fair Ladies, the host and hostess, absent friends, the guests, together and in turn. If there is a lull in the drinking or if the party seems to be falling into sections with people talking too exclusively to neighbors, there are drinking songs to bring them together again.

One of these is a simple affair in which A fills B's glass, while the company sings, and when B has emptied the glass he fills C's, and so on round the table, the bottle passing from hand to hand. Another song starts: "All those born in January, stand up, stand up and drink." When they have done so the chorus goes on to February, and so through each month of the year. When December is reached people are usually in the mood to return to January and go through it all again.

A song called "*Tcharichka,*" "The Silver Cup," is slightly more elaborate. A glass is presented ceremoniously to one of the guests with an invocation, sung as a solo: "Here is a silver cup on a golden tray . . . Whoever drinks from it will have good health. Drink and enjoy good fortune, our dear Nina Constantinovna—or Mikhail Nicolaevitch or Pavel Andrianovitch—etc., etc."

The honored one takes the glass and empties it while the company sings "Drink it up, drink it up!" and then, "She has drunk it, she has drunk it! *Na zdaroviyi!* Good health!" with which they also empty their glasses.

PANCAKE DAY

[Maslyanitza]

Seven weeks before Easter the Great Fast—Lent—begins. It continues until midnight on Easter Saturday.

The date of the Russian Easter varies but is usually a couple of weeks after ours. From time to time it coincides with Easter in the Western Church.

During the Great Fast strict Orthodox Russians eat nothing but vegetables and vegetable oils, which is severe discipline for a healthy Russian appetite, but people can break themselves in gradually through the Butter Fast or Little Fast, which is observed for a week before the Great Fast. During this week fish and dairy products are allowed but no meat.

Gastronomically speaking, the most important outcome of this Butter Fast is the invention of *blini* or pancakes. They are said to go back to pagan Russia, to the time when the present Christian Easter was the Spring Festival and round flat cakes were made as representations of the sun, returning after the winter darkness.

Blini are smaller and thicker than Western pancakes and may be of wheat, rye or buckwheat flour. The main difference from ours is that they are made with yeast, which gives a wonderful lightness. In the old days in Russia—and still in country districts—heavy cast-iron frying pans were kept specially and used for nothing else, sometimes shaped like a clover leaf to take three pancakes at the same time, or with two round "leaves." *Blini* can be made very successfully with an ordinary frying pan on top of the stove or with an electric fry pan which you can use at the table. Do not be discouraged if your first efforts are not entirely successful. The Russians have a saying, "*Piervii blin komon* . . ." "The first pancake is always a lump."

Blini may be eaten any time during the Little Fast and as often as you like, but most people have one big pancake party toward the end of the week, usually the Sunday before the Great Fast begins.

These parties are quite unlike the Western Pancake Day. The *blini* are eaten with caviar, anchovies, herrings, salted salmon, any kind of fish, and served with plenty of sour cream and melted butter.

There are no *zakuski* at a *blini* party. The fish, sour cream and butter are set out on the dining room table where the guests sit waiting. In the kitchen, spoonfuls are ladled out from an immense pot of liquid dough, poured into a hot buttered frying pan and as the *blini* are cooked, they are piled on a plate and sent to the table where they are seized by the guests, spread with fish, drenched with sour cream and washed down with vodka. Even those who have no intention of keeping the Great Fast eat and drink as though this were their last chance.

In the early stages of the party each pile of *blini* coming from the kitchen is greeted with eager cries and quickly demolished but as time passes and the toasts become more frequent, the voices rise and the caviar and salmon disappear, the consumption slows down until at last saturation point is reached.

Vodka is a help in neutralizing the cream and fats and is the only drink possible with such a meal. For a pancake party, work on the basis that 1 cup of liquid (milk and water combined) makes enough pancakes for 1 person.

Russian Pancakes

[Blini]

3 eggs
1 ounce fresh (compressed) yeast
¼ cup warm water
2 cups lukewarm water
1 teaspoon salt
1 tablespoon sugar
2–2½ cups plain flour
2 cups milk
Butter for frying

Separate the egg yolks and whites. Dissolve the yeast in ¼ cup warm water. Add the rest of the water, egg yolks, salt and sugar. Mix well together, add the flour and beat thoroughly.

Beat the egg whites stiff, add to the mixture, folding in carefully, and allow the dough to rise until it doubles itself in bulk, about 2–2½ hours.

Boil the milk and pour it into the dough while still boiling hot. Mix fast and well. Cover the mixing bowl and allow dough to rise for 1 hour, without touching it. It should become full of small bubbles. Do not mix or stir before cooking.

Heat a frying pan and brush it with melted butter, or just put in half a teaspoon of butter. Using a ladle, carefully scoop out about half a cup of dough. It should be taken from round the edges of the bowl so that the rest of the mixture is not disturbed. Pour it from the ladle onto the hot frying pan and cook on one side until the top is almost completely done; then put a small piece of butter in the center of the pancake, turn it over and cook for a few more minutes. Remove to an oven-proof plate and keep hot in the oven while you make the next *blin*. Repeat the process until all the dough is cooked, piling the pancakes one upon the other. *4 servings*

EASTER

[Pascha]

At the end of the Great Fast comes Easter, the biggest festival in the Russian year, even more important than Christmas. It has been described by many Russian writers, and emigrés all over the world celebrate it, even in countries where Easter marks the beginning of autumn instead of spring.

Orthodox Russians, no matter where, observe the traditional practice of Easter breakfast after midnight mass at their church or cathedral. Since the festivities go on all night, those who do not have to be at the church early to sing in the choir or perform some other service, usually sleep beforehand. By eleven o'clock the cathedral and its grounds are crowded with waiting people, each holding a candle. Some talk quietly, others are silent, their faces sad, their thoughts far away. The atmosphere is subdued. It is a beautiful and moving scene—the clear night with its sparkling stars, the little wavering flames of the candles shining up into the pale faces.

As the hours pass the crowd increases and by midnight the surrounding streets are filled with parked cars. At the doors of the cathedral a steady stream makes its way in and out of the building. Inside, the altar and ikons blaze with candles. The heat is stifling. Men and women in their best clothes, children, old *babushkas* with scarves over their heads, all carrying candles, press slowly toward the center of the church where the ikon of the dead Christ is lying, bend down and kiss it, then push their way out again, stopping to greet friends or halted by the density of the crowd.

On the last moments of Easter Saturday the ikon of Christ is carried behind the altar screen; then at midnight the bells ring out, the altar gates are opened and the bishops and priests come out, dressed in white. With acolytes swinging censers, followed by the singing choir and the worshipers with their lighted candles, the bishops, priests and deacons file out of the church. The procession circles the building, stopping at each of the four corners, north, south, east and west, then back to the entrance.

"*Christos Voskresi!* Christ is Risen!"
The censers are swung. The incense rises.
"*Christos Voskresi! Christos Voskresi!*"

Mourning is over. Christ is risen. The cry goes up all round. Everyone turns to his or her neighbor, no matter whom, saying "Christ is risen!" "*Wo istinu Voskres!*" ("He is risen indeed!") the neighbor replies and they kiss three times, on the right cheek, left cheek and on the lips.

The procession reenters the church but now the crowd begins to disperse. People move off in their cars, on foot, in groups. There is a change of mood, of tempo. Voices ring out, car engines start up and soon the great gathering has melted away, gone to their own or to friends' houses for the Easter breakfast. For the really strict Orthodox Russian this breaks the fast which began on Pancake Day, but even those who have denied themselves nothing during Lent are eager for the meal, for one goes to the service on an empty stomach.

In some houses the feast continues for 36 hours, in shifts, the first session starting immediately after church, about 1 A.M., the second a late lunch on Easter Sunday, with finally, for those who can manage it, an evening supper. On the table are all the foods forbidden during the Fast . . . hams and poultry, brawns and aspics, every kind of *zakuski*. There is less fish than usual, since people are rather tired of it by the end of Lent, and piles of brightly painted hard-cooked eggs are arranged on stands among the dishes. Everyone takes one of these Easter eggs and laughingly cracks the shell by knocking it against his neighbor's egg. Since the decorations are done with food coloring the eggs can be eaten with the *zakuski*.

The main features of the Easter table are the traditional *kulich* and *pascha*, which emigré Russians continued to make during the years when church festivals were no longer celebrated in their native land. There is no recipe for Easter *kulich* or *pascha* in some of the modern Soviet cookbooks but the older exile housewives have passed the recipes on to the younger generation and they are still made all over the world by Russians at Easter.

Good *pascha* is smooth, light and fine, a pyramid of cream cheese impregnated with dried fruits and nuts. Beside it on the table are the *kulichi*, domed cylinders of rich sweet bread with fruit, standing upright like little Byzantine towers. To eat *kulich* the top is cut off and slices taken from the middle, then the top put back to prevent dryness, for it stays on the table long after Easter—traditionally for 40 days, until Trinity.

Easter breakfasts are the nicest of all Russian parties. There is an air of excitement in starting at one o'clock in the morning and in the contrast between the subdued waiting at the cathedral and the sense of happiness and liberation that follows, for though someone is sure to lapse into a Dostoevsky mood sooner or later the atmosphere is joyful. No one seeing these people so wholeheartedly enjoying themselves would guess that next day some of them, no longer young, will be working at machines in factories or at menial jobs in hospitals, living a hard and circumscribed life until the next time there is a party.

Easter Menu

Hostesses who are going to church on Easter night do all their preparations for the party beforehand. The whole meal is cold, so hams and poultry can be cooked in advance. The *pascha* and *kulichi* are made a couple of days ahead and the Easter eggs are hard-cooked and painted with food coloring. (We suggest allowing 8 dozen eggs for the party, for decorated eggs, *zakuski*, cakes, *kulichi* and *pascha*.)

A suggested menu for about 10 people could include:

Zakuski:

Sprats
Smoked Eel*
Anchovies
Marinaded Fresh Fish in Tomato Sauce*
Decorated Hard-cooked Eggs

Meat:

Home-made Ham*
Roast Duck (or Goose) with Apples*
Chicken and Vegetable Salad*
Veal Brawn*

Sweets:

*Pascha**
*Kulich**
Pavlova Meringue Cream Cake*
Marinaded Fruits*

Drinks:

Vodka
Zubrowka
Wine
Cognac
Liqueurs
Coffee
Russian Tea

Kulich

Kulich is a tall cylindrical loaf with a domed top and stands upright on its base. It can be baked successfully in a 2-pound dried-milk, shortening or coffee can with the top cut off smoothly. For a specially big *kulich* use an 8-pound can; for very small loaves, the 1-pound size.

3 ounces fresh (compressed) yeast
1 cup warm water
2½ cups milk
1½ pounds sugar
1½ teaspoons salt
4 pounds plain flour
12–15 egg yolks (depending on size)
Few drops lemon extract
2 vanilla beans or vanilla extract to taste
½ teaspoon nutmeg
1 pound golden raisins
½ pound glacéed pineapple or cherries, diced
¼ pound candied orange peel
½ pound chopped almonds
1 pound butter
Butter to grease cake pans
Fine bread crumbs for cake pans

Preheat oven to 250° F.

Dissolve the yeast in 1 cup of warm water. Slightly warm the milk, put it into a bowl, add ½ pound of the sugar, the salt and yeast. Add 1½ pounds of the flour, beat well with a wooden spoon and leave to rise. In the meantime blend the rest of the sugar and egg yolks together, add the lemon extract, vanilla and nutmeg. If using vanilla beans, scrape out the center with a spoon or knife and mix in thoroughly with a little sugar.

Prepare the fruit and almonds. When the dough has doubled itself in size, melt the butter but do not overheat—just warm it. Add it to the dough, mix it in, then add the sugar and egg-yolk mixture. Mix again. Add half the remaining flour. Mix. Add the rest of the flour. The dough should now be quite firm, too firm to mix with a spoon, so work with your hand or even clenched fist, pushing and pummeling it for as long as you like—the longer the better. It should not stick to the hand at all when it is ready.

Add the fruit and nuts, working them in carefully so they do not break up. Cover with a clean cloth and stand in a warm place, out of drafts, until the dough doubles itself in size (2–3 hours).

Butter the 2-pound cans and sprinkle them with fine bread crumbs. When the dough has risen, fill one-third of each can, leaving room for rising. Stand for 30 minutes.

Bake in a slow oven for 1½–2 hours, until a long wooden cake tester comes out dry. The can must stand on its base in the oven.

Cover a soft pillow with grease-proof paper. Take the *kulich* from the oven and leave it in its can for 10 minutes; then slide it out carefully on its side on the pillow. Roll it gently from side to side every few minutes to preserve its shape. If left too long on one side it will lose its roundness. Do not try to stand it up until it is completely cool.

To serve, cut off the top, take slices from the *kulich*, then put the top back to prevent dryness. *This quantity of dough will fill 4 two-pound cans*

Pascha

Many countries have cottage cheese sweets and desserts; there are Italian *ricotta* recipes, French hot and cold cottage cheese creations, German and Austrian cheese cakes. It is possible that Russian *pascha* derives from one of these but it far surpasses them all.

For a really good *pascha* only the very best of materials should be used and there must be no skimping. It is rather an extravagant recipe but since it is usually made only once a year Russian housewives do not try to economize, for when it is well made it must be one of the most delicious sweets ever invented.

It is made with and without cooking; without fruit; with almonds only; with fruit and no almonds; or with both fruit and almonds. Uncooked *pascha* is far softer and finer than the cooked version.

1 *pound fresh* unsalted *cottage cheese, not too moist*
½ *pound* unsalted *butter*
½ *pound fine granulated sugar*
4 *egg yolks*
Vanilla to taste
1 *pound mixed golden raisins, glacéed pineapple, cherries, angelica and almonds . . . all chopped*

Put the cottage cheese through a very fine sieve.

In another bowl, cream the butter, sugar and egg yolks together until all the sugar has dissolved. Add vanilla and, gradually, the cottage cheese. Mix well, add fruit and almonds and mix them in lightly.

If you have a pyramid *pascha* mold line it with a damp cloth, leaving enough to cover the top. Put in the mixture, cover with the cloth and a small board and put a 2-pound weight to press on it for 24 hours.

When ready, unmold onto a dish or compote, with the pointed side up, and serve.

If there is no pyramid mold, use a colander lined with a damp cloth or a large clean lined flowerpot, also covered and weighted. Do not use ordinary basins for if the pressed-out moisture cannot escape the *pascha* will be soggy and start to separate.

A colander gives a round *pascha,* a flowerpot gives a slightly chimney-shaped one; but if you want the traditional pyramid and cannot get the wooden mold with detachable sides, shape into a pyramid with a knife, after removing from colander or flowerpot. *8–10 servings*

Cooked Pascha
[Pascha Variyonaia]

2 pounds unsalted fresh cottage cheese
6 egg yolks
1 pound sugar
1 pound unsalted butter
Vanilla to taste
1 cup sour cream
½ pound chopped almonds

Wrap the cottage cheese in a cloth and put it between two boards with a weight on top for 6–8 hours, then put it through a fine sieve.

Cream the yolks, sugar and butter, add the vanilla, then the sour cream. Mix in with the cottage cheese. Add the almonds. Put into the top of a double boiler, heat almost to boiling point but do not boil. Let it cool, put into a mold lined with a clean damp cloth, cover and set under a 2-pound weight for 24 hours. *8–10 servings*

CHRISTMAS
[Rozjedestvo]

By comparison with Easter, the Russian Christmas is a quiet affair, mainly devoted to children and family and not celebrated in the lavish way that greets the end of Lent. It is held later than in the Western Church, on January 7, and strict Orthodox Russians fast for six weeks beforehand. This is a completely vegetarian fast and while it lasts there must be no parties or gay gatherings. It is broken on Christmas Eve, when the first star appears, with a traditional dish called *Kutija.* After this the tree is decorated; then, on Christmas Day the table is set for the family dinner.

A typical Christmas menu includes Goose with Apples*, duck, ham, preceded by many *zakuski.* The sweets are usually cookies called *Hvorost*—Branches*; a fruit cake called *Mazurka**, nuts and dried fruits, candies and some kind of *tort,* served with coffee or tea.

During Christmas no one need wait for an invitation to visit friends, and people drop in on each other throughout the holiday, to drink tea and exchange greetings.

Kutija, with which the fast is broken, is made in different ways in different parts of Russia. In the south it is made with boiled rice and raisins, honey and walnuts; in Central Russia, with cooked whole wheat, honey, poppy seed, golden raisins and walnuts. This same mixture is also served at Orthodox funerals when it is dealt out to the mourners from a great dish. It is an ancient Slavonian custom.

Kutija

*1 cup hot Boiled Rice**
½ cup sugar
1 tablespoon honey
½ cup raisins

When the water has been drained off the boiled rice, mix in the sugar and honey. Turn onto a serving dish and scatter raisins on top. This makes about 2 cups of *Kutija. 4 servings*

NAME DAY

[Iminine]

All Orthodox Russians are christened after saints. The only names permitted to them are listed in a book kept by the priest.

This means that as well as having a birthday to celebrate they also have a Name Day, or patron saint's day. This is a more important occasion than a birthday because it is also a religious holy day. Strict Orthodox believers go to church before their party to honor their saint. Others content themselves with the party.

Due to the number of saints in the Russian calendar, *Iminine* parties seem to occur with great frequency.

These parties are often very elaborate, with many rich dishes, but the old traditional *Iminine* food was a *pirog* or pie. *Pirog* is still included in all Name Day menus and may contain meat, fish, cabbage or any other filling. It could even be like the *pirog* described by Gogol, which had four corners, each with a different filling—one containing a sturgeon's cheeks, another mushrooms, onions and *kasha*, and so on. At *Iminine* parties the *pirog* is preceded by *zakuski* and the first three toasts are always drunk to the guest of honor whose Name Day is being celebrated.

Though modern *Iminine* parties are usually organized, with people invited in advance, the old custom was to keep open house, when anyone could drop in for a piece of pie or *Krendel**, a special sweet loaf, or a cup of tea. Sometimes the callers started to arrive in the morning and the visits went on all day. In this, as in all traditional Russian customs, the emphasis is on hospitality, on opening one's house to friends and strangers, on sharing one's food, drink, gaiety and good fellowship.

WEDDINGS

[Svadiba]

Orthodox Russian weddings are quite unlike their Western counterparts, not only in the spectacular ceremony and magnificent singing but in the fact that they are often held on Sundays (Tuesdays, Thursdays and Saturdays and church fast days are forbidden for weddings); and that the congregation remains standing for the whole of the service.

In pagan Russia, among certain tribes, the bridegroom had to kidnap his bride; in others he had to pay the clan for her. Later, this payment was replaced by a gift from the bridegroom to the bride or her parents.

After Christianity came, engagements and weddings were blessed by the church but at first this custom was only observed by princes and *boyars* (hereditary noblemen). Up till the fifteenth century the people, especially in country districts, required only official recognition of the marriage by the clan or community.

Under Byzantine law marriage took place at an early age. In the eighth century it was fifteen for men, thirteen for women; in the ninth century it was fourteen for men and twelve for women.

In the old days parents made the matches and arranged the marriages and there are still Russian women living who never saw their bridegrooms before the ceremony. This often happened when the couple lived in different districts.

Though life has changed so much, certain customs still survive and many young emigré Russians follow the traditional procedure. The engagement is not announced with a ring and photographs in the paper but an agreement is made between the families, in the Russian manner; and though the parents do not make the choice, their blessing is asked. This is given before an ikon, the young pair kneeling before the parents.

Three or four weeks before the ceremony the marriage is announced in church, and a week before, the engaged pair take communion together. They do not meet for 24 hours before they arrive at church on the wedding day. The bridegroom should not see the wedding dress.

The bride comes to the church with her veil over her face and is met at the entrance by the priest and bridegroom. In a brief service their engagement is publicly confirmed. This may be done any time during the engagement but is usual just before the wedding. The bride stands on the left, the bridegroom on the right. Joining their hands together the priest offers up a special prayer for them; then the bride's veil is put back and the party moves into the center of the church for the main service.

This is beautiful, bizarre and fascinating, with superb music and singing. The priest gives both bride and groom a lighted candle to hold during the service. Rings are exchanged three times; the sacramental wine is sipped and finally the priest leads the couple three times round the center of the church.

During the ceremony the groomsmen take turns to hold heavy crowns over the heads of bride and groom.

There are no pews in a Russian church and the friends and relations stand round on both sides, many in tears. Usually the parents are not present. They wait at the reception to greet the bride and groom with an ikon and the traditional Bread and Salt of Happiness Cake*.

One mother offers the bread and salt—a little round loaf with a small salt cellar in the top—and the other, holding an ikon, blesses and welcomes the newlyweds. After the blessing the bread and salt are tasted. This is symbolic of cleaning away past sins, of starting a fresh life together, of health and happiness.

Before the guests sit down to the wedding breakfast there is a champagne toast to the married couple and then the party gets under way. The long table is covered with food and drink. The wedding cake is an immense sweet affair which the bride and bridegroom cut together and pass round.

None of it is taken home to sleep on or posted off to absent friends. Every scrap is demolished on the spot.

The banquet is long and hilarious. Among the speeches and endless toasts are constant cries of "*Gorko! Gorko!* (Bitter!)" from the guests. This means that the food is bitter and the bride and groom must kiss to make it sweeter.

The length of the church ceremony and the fact that everyone stands up through it does not dampen enthusiasm. It only increases appetites.

The newlyweds are not expected to go early and often stay till the end of the party. Before leaving, the bride throws her flowers to her bridesmaids and there is a noisy farewell. If there is still food and drink left the guests return to the table after the departure and carry on till all is finished.

Wedding Cake

There is no special recipe for wedding cake. It is just any rich sweet cake or *tort* such as given in the Cake chapter of this book.

Happiness Cake

[Hliep s Soliyu]

(Bread and Salt offered by the mothers to the newlyweds after the ceremony)

1 cup butter
4 tablespoons sugar
1 teaspoon salt
3 eggs
Vanilla extract to taste
1 cup milk
1 ounce fresh (compressed) yeast
¼ cup warm water
3½ cups plain flour
Little nutmeg
Butter and bread crumbs for baking pan
1 egg for brushing
Extra salt for salt container

Preheat oven to 350° F.

Soften the butter, then cream with the sugar and add the salt, eggs, vanilla extract, then the milk. Dissolve the yeast in ¼ cup warm water and add to mixture. With wooden spoon beat in the flour and nutmeg, beating the dough for 5–10 minutes. Leave it to rise. Butter and bread crumb a round cake pan, not too deep. When the dough has doubled itself in bulk put it carefully into the cake pan and leave for 10–15 minutes. Brush it with beaten egg and bake for 30–35 minutes. Test with cake tester. If it comes out clean, the cake is done.

When cooked leave for 10 minutes in the pan, then remove and cool on a rack.

On the wedding day put a little container to hold the salt in the center top of the cake.

This cake is used to welcome loved and respected friends arriving to stay. Bread and salt are old Russian symbols of respect and allegiance, as mentioned in the Russian epic of *Sadko, the Rich Merchant of Novgorod:*

> To the Tsar beyond the sea
> I have never paid tribute or duty . . .
> And in the blue Khvalinsk sea
> I never threw bread and salt.

PICNICS

[Picnics]

Russian picnics are splendid and memorable. No time is wasted on long hot drives. The nearest, shadiest, prettiest place is chosen and quickly strewn with cushions, rugs, umbrellas, bottles of vodka, jars of *shaslik,* skewers, baskets of *zakuski,* salads, *pirogs* and *torts.* The quiet country air is soon shattered with exuberant cries, Russian songs, the sound of axes, shouts and arguments about the best place to build the fire. The first thing is to find somewhere to keep the vodka cool, preferably a stream or pool; then all must have a drink and a snack to revive them after the drive, no matter how short. The ax-man, fire-builders, cook and onlookers must be fortified. *Zakuski* are unpacked; the meat and onions for *shaslik* taken from their marinade and threaded on the skewers. It is thirsty work and another round of vodka is needed; then another, while you wait for the fire to burn down to the right state for cooking *shaslik.* The feast, when it finally starts, is long and varied and followed by somnolence, arguments, declaiming of poems and songs.

Shaslik, the great picnic food, is the Caucasian name for cooking on skewers. It is very similar to Turkish and Persian *şiş kebab* and the Greek *souvlakia* but the meat is cut into bigger pieces and the skewers are larger. The Caucasians use their swords. Each country claims to have invented this wonderful way of cooking meat; the Turks say the Greeks took it from them, the Russians say the Turks took it from the Caucasians, the Greeks say it was theirs to start with. In the *Iliad* Homer describes the Greeks cooking pieces of lamb on skewers outside the walls of Troy; yet Troy is in Asia Minor (Turkey) and the Turks came from the land of Touran, beyond the Caucasus and the Caspian Sea. Whoever invented it, it is a masterpiece; and though it is now served in restaurants all over the world it is always best eaten out of doors, with plenty of red wine, surrounded by the scents of charcoal smoke and cooking lamb.

In the different regions of Russia, *shaslik* varies in proportions and use of meat. Abkhasian *shaslik* is made of fat mutton and sheep's liver cut into pieces; Georgian *shaslik* of meat and onion, without liver; Uzbekistan *shaslik* is cooked on wooden skewers instead of metal; Baku *shaslik* is of lamb or mutton cut into 1-ounce pieces. Normally the meat is marinaded beforehand in lemon juice but in southern Russia pomegranate juice is used. This could have come from Persia, where pomegranate juice is used for this and other dishes.

Lamb Cooked on Skewers

[Shaslik]

6–7 pounds lamb leg chops or 7-pound leg of lamb
Salt and pepper
1½ pounds onions
Juice 6–7 lemons, depending on size. There must be enough to cover the meat

Optional: 2 pounds tomatoes, 6 green peppers, 1 pound bacon

The night before the picnic, cut out all the fat and bones from the meat and cut the meat into pieces about 2 inches square by ½ inch thick. Salt and pepper them and put them into a big jar of glass or earthenware or anything that is not affected by the acid of lemon juice. Slice the onions and put them in the jar between layers of the meat. Pour the lemon juice over it all and leave all night. (The jar should be full of alternate layers of onion and meat.)

Tomatoes cut in quarters, strips of green peppers and sections of bacon are sometimes added at the last minute, not marinaded overnight with the meat. To prepare for cooking, thread meat, bacon, onion, peppers, tomatoes alternately on the skewers till each skewer is full.

Cook over hot charcoal or glowing embers, turning the skewers so the meat cooks evenly on all sides. *8 servings*

Marinaded fruit goes well with *shaslik,* which is really a meal in itself, but Russian picnics being what they are there will probably be many *zakuski,* mainly canned and smoked fish, salami and other sausages, all easy to transport. All sorts of *pirogs* and *piroshki,* breads and *torts* are popular picnic foods and *Forshmack v Kalache*—Beef and Herring in Bread Crust*. Potato salad, cold pot roast and cold Homemade Ham* may be included and the drinks are usually vodka, brandy and red wine.

RUSSIAN DRINKS

(RUSSKIYE NAPITKI)

"Drinking is the joy of the Rus'. He cannot exist without that pleasure," said St. Vladimir, explaining to the Moslem emissaries why his country could not embrace Islam, which prohibits alcohol.

Love of strong drink and ability to take it in large quantities is a Russian characteristic that has often astonished foreigners. Brillat-Savarin once remarked that "the ration of a sick Russian, in 1815, would have made a strong porter of the Paris markets drunk."

Most non-Russians regard vodka as Russia's national drink; yet this much-loved spirit is comparatively modern. In ancient times, even the Kievan period, when Kiev was capital, there was no distilled liquor. It was not till the fourteenth century that the Russians learned the art of distilling from grain, from Genovese living in the Crimea.

The oldest traditional Slav drinks are *kvass* and *med* (mead). They are both mentioned in an early fifth-century account of a Byzantine envoy traveling across Russia from Constantinople to visit Attila the Hun, but appear to date from much earlier.

Mead, which came from Scandinavia, was very popular in Kievan Russia and was drunk freely by both monks and laymen. The Ancient Chronicles describe St. Vladimir ordering 300 kettles of mead for the opening of a new church, and mention a twelfth-century prince who kept 500 casks of mead in his cellar.

Mead contains honey and honeyed drinks never lost their popularity with the Russians. Nineteenth-century travelers describe mead sold at railway stations in old Dutch or German silver beakers. There were several varieties, sweet, dry or peppered. Modern Russians are fond of a rather similar drink called *Brajka,* made from fermented wheat and honey. At funerals an old custom was to hand round a mixture of mead, beer, wine and rum. The mourners stood while the priests recited the final prayers, then all drank to the departed soul. The mixture was called *Trisna,* after the name of this ancient Slavonian funeral ceremony.

Beer (*Pivo*). This has been drunk in Russia for many centuries and in early days was considered part of the basic diet. St. Sergius of Radonezh, subjecting himself to mortification and prayer in his cell near Moscow, is said to have fasted so severely that "he denied himself even beer."

Kvass is a very early Slavonic drink. It is mentioned in A.D. 100 and is still widely drunk.

Oldest of all, though not Slavonic, is the Tartar drink called *Koumiss.* It is so ancient that it is mentioned in Herodotus, and is made from mare's milk. It is still drunk in the Kirghiz region of the U.S.S.R. and is highly nutritious. It is often recommended for invalids, especially consumptives. Traditionally it is made either in smoked horse-skins or in wooden tubs, and an *eau de vie* can be produced by fermenting it. (The Caucasians also make a drink from fermented camel's milk.)

Ten champagne quart bottles of *koumiss* are said to supply all the nourishment needed by a strong fully grown adult.

Wine. (*Vino*) The Russians learned to drink wine from the Greeks through their contact with Byzantium, before the Mongol invasion. Wine-drinking was also closely connected with Christian church ritual. During the Tartar domination, communciation was broken with the Eastern Empire and wine was no longer drunk; but the custom was revived in the time of the tsars. Greek wine was later replaced by Hungarian and finally French wines, introduced by Peter the Great, who also imported vines for growing in the Crimea.

Wine was made in Astrakhan as early as 1613 but though the grapes were excellent the wine was said to have a strange flavor, possibly from the goat skins in which it was kept.

Caucasian and Crimean wines and sherries soon became appreciated by foreigners. The best Soviet wines still come from these areas. Champagne is also made. Though certain Russians reject all drinks but vodka there are many who cannot resist champagne. This wine, usually associated with the more cosmopolitan aristocracy of tsarist days, was also appreciated by the nineteenth-century Kalmuck prince who entertained Alexandre Dumas:

"When we reached the dessert stage, the prince asked me to come to the window, glass in hand, to receive a toast from the Kalmucks still feasting outside. As I appeared they all rose to their feet, each with his wooden drinking vessel in one hand and a half-gnawed bone in the other, gave me a cheer and drank my health. The prince decided that my glass was too small for an adequate response, so he handed me a great horn bound with silver, poured into it a whole bottle of champagne, and though I am no drinker I managed to drain it in honor of his subjects, the 300 in the courtyard and their 11,000 fellow-serfs throughout his realm."

Vodka. Russians do not consider a meal complete without vodka, especially for the *zakuski* course. There is much to be said for the practice. The clean spirit, served icy cold, is the perfect accompaniment to smoked or salted fish, rich mayonnaise and sour cream dishes. It is always drunk neat. It is never sipped; it should be swallowed in one gulp and is served in glasses just big enough to hold this amount. Though it looks innocuous it is potent and quickly warms up the most frigid guest. The custom of drinking neat spirit in cold countries was probably designed for this purpose for it not only thaws out those who have traveled through the snow but breaks the social ice.

Vodka is drunk by women as well as men, though perhaps in smaller quantities. Some Russian restaurants supply free *zakuski* for their drinkers without loss, since the amount of liquor consumed pays for the food. A pretty custom was for the friends of a newly engaged man to spell out his fiancée's name in vodka glasses and expect him to drink them all to prove his love.

True vodka, which is made from wheat, is colorless and looks like water; but there are different varieties. (Gogol talks of "six different vodkas, surrounded by a necklace of *zakuski.*") Some of the best known are *zubrowka,* from Poland, pale almond-green with a faint aromatic scent from the grass infused in it; *vishniowka,* cherry vodka, which is red;

lemon or orange vodka in which peel is infused; and pepper and strong pepper vodka for those who can take them.

Kvass

This is non-alcoholic, made from black bread and yeast. It is the great drink of the Russian peasant and is frequently mentioned in Russian literature. It is harmless and is used in cold soups, such as *Okroshka.* In summer it is sold in restaurants and in the streets from small tanks.

When making *kvass* put it in the refrigerator as soon as bottled, using corks, not screw-in stoppers. If it is not chilled at once it will go on fermenting and if the seething liquid cannot blow its cork it will shatter the bottle.

1 pound dried-out sliced black bread
24 cups boiling water
3 cups sugar
2 ounces fresh yeast (compressed)
½ cup golden raisins

Put the bread into a big saucepan or earthenware crock and pour the boiling water over it. Allow it to cool until lukewarm, then carefully squeeze the liquid from the bread, straining through a muslin cloth so that no bread comes through, which would cloud the *kvass.* Add the sugar and yeast. Mix, cover and leave for 10–12 hours.

Pour the *kvass* into clean bottles, add 2 or 3 raisins to each, cork and tie down. Put into the refrigerator *immediately* and keep there until needed.

This is the normal *kvass* but there are other drinks which might be regarded as variations—*Yablochinkvas* (Cider); *Grusheviikvas* (Perry—made from pears); *Malinovoi,* from raspberries. *Makes about 10 bottles*

Fruit-wine Liqueurs

Some of the Russian women make very pleasant home-made liqueurs, from mulberries, raspberries, loganberries, cherries, etc., and though perhaps sometimes they are inclined to be rather sweet, the best of them make a good accompaniment to black coffee.

Half fill a ½-gallon bottle or jar with berries; add sugar till the jar is full. Cover and leave to ferment, for 6–8 weeks. The berries should settle down into the juice so that no bubbles remain.

Put the berries through a fine sieve, squeezing out the juice. Filter everything through a thin layer of cottonwool or a very fine cloth. The juice should be quite clear. Add alcohol to the strength you wish, using vodka, brandy or cognac. The easiest way to filter is to put a funnel into the neck of the bottle, lay cottonwool in it and pour the liquid through from the fermenting jar.

Cruchons and Punches

In Georgia, where some of the best U.S.S.R. red and white wines are made and drunk, *Cruchon* is a popular summer drink. It is really a delicate fruit punch.

Caucasian Fruit Punch

[Kavkaskii Cruchon]

1 pound fruit—peaches, apricots, cherries, pineapple, etc.
1 bottle sweet white wine
1 ounce cognac
Peel from ¼ lemon, cut in strips
Rind ½ cucumber, cut in strips

Cut up the fruit, removing stones, and half fill a large glass jug. Mix together the rest of the ingredients and pour over. Chill thoroughly. Drink the punch and eat the fruit afterward. *Makes approximately 1 quart*

Fantasy Fruit Punch

[Fantasia Cruchon]

1 pound any fruit in season
1 bottle white port
1 bottle madeira
3 ounces cognac
Sugar to taste—the quantity depends on whether fruit is sweet or not
Juice ½ lemon

Chop up the fruit. Mix together other ingredients and pour over. Leave for at least half an hour, preferably longer, in the refrigerator, and drink very cold. *Makes approximately 2 quarts*

Hot Punch

[Goriatchi Punsh]

3 ounces brandy
1 tablespoon confectioners' powdered sugar
Dash lemon juice
3 ounces boiling water

Mix all ingredients together and drink hot. This quantity makes punch for *one person,* so should be multiplied according to number of servings needed.

Hot Milk Punch

[Molochni Punsh, Goriachi]

1 ounce brandy or any chosen liqueur
1 teaspoon confectioners' powdered sugar
3½ ounces milk
Nutmeg

Put brandy and sugar into a glass. Boil the milk and pour over while hot. Dust with nutmeg. This quantity makes enough for *one person.*

Both this and Hot Punch* would be improved by using cognac instead of brandy.

Russian Tea
[Russki Chai]

Like vodka and *kvass*, tea is one of Russia's national beverages and few homes are without a samovar or tea urn. These are also found in public tearooms, tea gardens, even cemeteries.

Because of their trade and contact with China, the people in the east of Russia early became used to the highest quality Chinese tea. They drank brick tea, and yellow tea which is pale and has a delicious flavor, though said to be bad for the nerves. Yellow tea, which is taken after dinner instead of coffee, was much preferred to brick tea, which is made from tea leaves that have been steamed, crushed in a mortar and made into cakes.

To the Russians, the samovar is more than a tea urn; it is a symbol of hospitality and family life. Tolstoy calls it a "sacred shrine." In big households, dispensing tea was quite a ritual.

Though many modern samovars are wired for electricity, the traditional model is heated with charcoal, contained in a central cylinder. The tea is made in a pot and stood on top of the samovar and the hot water singing inside is drawn off through a little tap. About half an inch of very strong tea is poured into the cup or glass—men drink tea from glasses, women from cups—and the rest filled with hot water. It is usually drunk with lemon, but some people put a spoonful of jam[1]—raspberry, blackberry, black currant—into the tea

[1] In Russian jam the fruit is left intact, not mashed up, because it is not intended for spreading on bread. It is eaten with a teaspoon from a little saucer.

and a few slices of apple on top, or drink it with honey, cream or milk.

This custom of adding fruit, jam, etc., is a relic of an ancient Chinese practice which the Russians learned from the Chinese *caravanserais.* The tea was boiled with rice, ginger, salt, orange peel, spices, milk and sometimes onions. Some Tibetan, Nepalese and Mongolian tribes still make a similar syrup; and the Kalmucks and Kisghiz of the steppes think highly of brick tea, as poor Dumas discovered: ". . . an abominable beverage . . . made from a piece of tea-brick from China, boiled in a saucepan with milk, butter and salt."

TYPICAL RUSSIAN MENUS

(RUSSKIYE MENU)

BREAKFAST

Omelet with Sour Cream Sauce
Cottage Cheese Spread with Caraway Seeds
Toast
Tea or Coffee

Scrambled Egg with Frankfurters
Yoghurt
Toast
Tea or Coffee

Breakfast Semolina
Sweet Cottage Cheese
Toast
Tea or Coffee

LUNCH

Noodles, Sailor Style
Pumpkin Pudding

Pilaff *with Eggs and Ham*
Sweet Cottage Cheese Paste

Crab and Rice Croquettes
Baked Fish with Egg

Apple Soup
Macaroni Baked with Fruit

Fried Pancake Pies
Branches *with tea*

DINNER

Zakuski
Fish Soup
Fish Kotlet *with Mushroom Sauce*
Cottage Cheese Patties

Zakuski
Fish Soup with Salted Cucumber
Fish Gratin
Apple Charlotte with Egg Sauce

Zakuski
Moscow Borsch
Pork Fillets with Apples
Kisel

Zakuski
Kidney and Cucumber Soup
Chicken Fillets in Bread Crumbs
Pancake Pies with Cottage Cheese

Zakuski
Georgian Soup
Chahohbili *of Chicken*
Rice Pudding with Kisel

Zakuski
Cold Kvass Soup with Crab Meat
Pot Roast in Aspic
Ice cream—Plombir

SPECIAL DINNERS OR PARTIES

Zakuski:
Salted Herring
Hot-smoked Fish
Smoked Salmon
Grilled Half-eggs
Stuffed Green Peppers
Liver Paste
Egg with Horseradish

Soup:
Cabbage Soup served with
Deep-fried Little Pies with Cabbage Filling

Meat:
Ham Cooked in Beer

Dessert:
Coffee Parfait
Sweet Cakes with Coffee

Zakuski:
Crab with Mayonnaise
Anchovies on Eggs
Fish in Aspic
Marinaded Fresh Fish in Tomato Sauce
Potato Salad
Fresh Spring Salad
Radishes in Sour Cream

Soup:
Spring Soup served with
Little Pies with Spring Onions and Egg Filling

Meat:
Roast Duck with Apples

Dessert:
Fruit Surprise
Pavlova Meringue Cream Cake with Coffee

SUPPLIES FOR RUSSIAN COOKING

A Russian housewife usually has in her store-cupboard or refrigerator some or all of the following, for everyday meals:

STAPLES:
kasha (buckwheat)
flour
sunflower or peanut oil
black bread
rye bread
noodles
rice
peppercorns
sesame seeds; poppy seeds; sunflower seeds
cloves
cinnamon
mustard
paprika

sugar
fine granulated sugar
confectioners' powdered sugar
honey
jams
horseradish—bought or homemade
dried mushrooms
acetic acid, used instead of vinegar

Canned Foods:

anchovies
sprats
sardines
kilkies (Norwegian anchovies)
caviar—red or black (must be kept in refrigerator)
canned soups
tomato purée
canned mushrooms
asparagus

Dairy Foods:

sour cream } bought or homemade
yoghurt }
cheeses
cottage cheese
eggs

Preserved Foods:

marinaded fruits and vegetables
pickled cucumbers
dried fruits and peel
salted herring
smoked and boiled ham

Meat and more perishable smoked fish are bought as needed. The fresh vegetables most frequently used are cabbage, potatoes, mushrooms, onions, green onions, squash, green and red peppers, tomatoes, cucumber, eggplant, carrots, beets.

The most popular herbs and flavorings are garlic, dill, parsley, bay leaves, chives.

Busy working wives probably keep ready-made deep-frozen *pelemeni* in the freezer and for unexpected visitors canned or frozen delicacies such as crab, Boeuf Stroganoff, etc.

COOKING EQUIPMENT

No special kitchen implements are needed. A set of skewers with wooden handles, such as sold for barbecues, will do for *shaslik*; a deep rather than wide pot, very big indeed, is best for making *borsch*, and you want some good sharp knives for filleting fish and chicken. Use coffee or shortening cans instead of the special mold for *baba* or *kulich*, and use a colander or flowerpot instead of the special wooden *pascha* mold.

Other necessary items are a pan for deep-frying; a good-sized pan for making *blini* (Russian pancakes); a saucepan big enough to boil *pelemeni* and a perforated spoon for lifting them out.

In the old days most of the cooking pots were of cast iron, with a few copper utensils, and wooden bowls and spoons were used. The typical Russian stove—*Russkaya Piechka*—was enormous, built into the wall with a hot plate—*pleeta*—in front, a baker's oven behind it and quite often a shelf above it where the servants, the very old or the very young liked to lie to keep warm.

For the Table

For Russian meals, everyone should have two plates, one slightly smaller than the other, and two forks. Plenty of small dishes for *zakuski* are essential. It is a good idea to collect serving dishes, platters and tureens of all kinds including old-fashioned compotes, which are useful for *torts* and cakes and marinaded fruits. Little forks of silver or mother of pearl are good for helping yourself to *zakuski*. Vodka glasses are an important item. They should be 1-ounce size, just big enough for one gulp.

For tea, a samovar is of course traditional, but emigrés who no longer possess one manage quite well without. For daily use, a modern samovar, wired for electricity, is the most practical.

INDEX